A Treatise on
The Fear of God

What it is and how it is distinguished from
that which is not so; also, whence it comes,
who has it, what the effects are, and what the
privileges are of those who have it in their hearts

by

John Bunyan
(author of *Pilgrim's Progress*)

Edited by Dr. Don Kistler

Soli Deo Gloria Publications
. . . for instruction in righteousness . . .

Soli Deo Gloria Publications
P.O. Box 451, Morgan, PA 15064
(412) 221-1901/FAX 221-1902
www.SDGbooks.com

*

A Treatise on the Fear of God was first published in
London in 1679. This Soli Deo Gloria reprint,
in which spelling, grammar,and formatting
changes have been made, is © 1999
by Soli Deo Gloria.

*

ISBN 1-57358-084-8

*

Fourth printing 2002

Contents

Introduction

by Maureen Bradley

"To a believing heart, God is all purity. His light is 'as the color of the terrible crystal,' of which Ezekiel writes. His brightness is so great that no man can approach unto it. We are so sinful that, when we get even a glimpse of the divine holiness, we are filled with fear, and we cry, with Job, 'I have heard of Thee by the hearing of the ear: but now mine eye seeth Thee. Wherefore I abhor myself, and repent in dust and ashes.' This is a kind of fear which we have need to cultivate, for it leads to repentance, and confession of sin, to aspirations after holiness, and to the utter rejection of all self-complacency and self-conceit."[1]

In this treatise Bunyan shows the fear of God is the constant description which the Scripture gives of true religion. It is the beginning of wisdom and the source of all happiness.

Proceeding from this foundational truth will flow a life of piety and grateful obedience. The starting point for the fear of God is a right view of who God is in His person, expressed in His attributes,

---

[1] Charles Spurgeon. *Spurgeon's Expository Encyclopedia* (Grand Rapids: Baker Book House, 1985), Vol. 7, p. 279.

and a right view of God in His presence, as seen in His transcendence and immanence correctly understood.

That there may be no error on this important subject, Bunyan has sought to clarify the definition of the fear of God by making several distinctions. He has distinguished between a filial fear of offending God (such as a child would have of displeasing a parent) and that fear a sinner has as he realizes that God is the infinitely Holy One before whom all sin is detestable and from whom he will incur wrath and punishment. There is the fear a subject holds for a benevolent king, as compared to the fear the demons have of God's great power and righteous judgment. A further distinction can be made between the fear of a slave to his master and the fear of a child to his father, as it relates to their response to the authority over them. There is the evangelical fear connected with seeking the Lord (Hosea 3:5) and the fear which stems from the dread and terror of fleeing God's righteous wrath (Revelation 6:16). True fear, the right kind of fear, saves and enlarges the soul.

As the effects and privileges of the fear of God are presented, it becomes evident that this grace is an artisan well from whence springs nurturing waters to vivify all other graces. Bunyan writes, "If you would have every grace that God has put into your souls grow and flourish into perfection, lay them to soak in this grace of fear, and do all in the exercise of it" (p. 146). Holy awe and reverence sweep over men as they perceive God's greatness. The vastness of God's works in nature can be seen in the panoramic view from a mountain top, and man's frailty known by standing in the midst of a storm surrounded by the Omnipotence's strength displayed in the lightening and thunder. God's providence proclaims His immutability and sovereignty as world leaders come and go, but God remains in all His absolute power. Before God's austere holiness and perfection, redeemed sinners shrink to nothing in lowly adoration and worship as they consider the great salvation which the Righteous Creator of the universe has provided. A high and hallowed worship of God will be the privilege of men and angels for all eternity. Indeed God "is greatly to be feared in the assembly of the saints, and to be had in reverence of all them that are about Him" (Psalm 89:7).

In applying this doctrine, Bunyan directs a sober examination to judge whether the fear of God dwells in a person or not, with characteristics given of those who do not fear God. "Two things are to be trembled at: the presence of God which fills all places, and the Word of God which reaches to all times."[2] However, our insufficient knowledge of these two things has caused a disrespectful casualness in our relationship to God. His exhortation to fear God includes motives to strengthen, ways to grow, and hindrances to this growth. He ends with the encouragement of why one is blessed if they fear God.

The following words of Matthew Henry summa-

---

[2] *Park Street Pulpit* (Grand Rapids: Baker Book House, 1990), Vol. 3, p. 326.

rize the comprehensive treatment Bunyan has provided on the fear of God: "Of all things that are to be
known this is most evident, that God is to be feared,
to be reverenced, served, and worshipped; this is so
the beginning of knowledge that those know nothing who do not know this."[3]

[3] *Matthew Henry's Commentary on the Whole Bible* (Iowa Falls:
World Bible Publishers), Vol. 3, p. 793.

Outline

C. *A fear of God which is good and godly, but only for a time:*
1. Is an effect of sound awakenings by the word of wrath which begets in the soul a sense of its right to eternal damnation.
2. Is wrought in the heart by the Spirit of God, working there at first as a Spirit of bondage to purposely put us in fear.
   a. Shows us by the law that we are in bondage to the law, the devil, death, and damnation.
   b. Holds us in sight and sense of our bondage-state so long as is meet we be held.
3. What this fear does in the soul:
   a. Causes a man to judge himself for sin and fall down before God.
   b. Condole and bewail his misery before God.
   c. Lie at God's footstool and puts his mouth in the dust.
   d. Cry to God for mercy.
   e. Cannot accept that support and succor others who are destitute will take up.
   f. Does not go away until the Spirit of God changes His ministration.
4. Ground work for this fear is good; fear of damnation:
   a. It is in sin.
   b. It has not faith in Christ but under the law.
   c. The wrath of God abides on it.

 L. *The least portion gives the privilege to be blessed with the greatest saint.*
  1. In esteem.
  2. Stature or young in years.
  3. In grace or gifts.
 M. *Holy Spirit has indicted a whole psalm to sing.*
 N. *Objection made and answered:*
  1. Objection: "Perfect love casteth our fear."
  2. Answered: Fear may be taken in several ways:
   a. Fear of the devils.
   b. Fear of reprobates.
   c. Fear that is wrought in the godly by the Spirit as the Spirit of bondage.

VI. The Use of This Doctrine
 A. *An examination of ourselves whether the fear of God is in us or not.*
  1. In general.
   a. No man brings this grace into the world with him.
   b. All other graces flow from this fear of God.
  2. In particular, propositions concerning those that fear not God:
   a. Those that are proud and of a high and lofty mind.
   b. Covetous.
   c. Riotous eaters of flesh.
   d. Liars.
   e. Cry unto Him for help in the time of calamity and when delivered return to their former rebellion.

b. The privileges that this grace lays you under.
c. The man who grows in this grace will escape those evils into which others will fall.
d. It will keep you in a conscientious performance of Christian duties.
e. A way to be wise.
f. It is seemly for the saints to fear and increase in the fear of God.
g. It is honorable to grow in this grace of fear.
h. Qualifies a man to be put in trust with heavenly and spiritual things, yea, with earthly things too.
i. Where it is not growing no grace thrives, nor duty done as it should be.
j. If you abound therein, it will give you great boldness with God and men.
k. May have your labors blessed to the saving of the souls of others.
l. To engage God to deliver you from many outward dangers, whoever falls therein.
m. The way to be delivered from errors and damnable opinions.
n. May come boldly to Jesus Christ to trust in Him for life.
o. God will own and acknowledge such to be His, whoever He rejects.
2. Ways how to grow in this fear of God:
a. Learn to distinguish fear in general.
b. Learn to distinguish fear in particular.

    c. Make conscience of which to entertain and cherish.

    d. Grow in the knowledge of the new covenant.

    e. Labor to keep evidences for heaven and salvation alive upon your heart.

    f. Set before your eyes on the being and majesty of God.

    g. Keep close to your conscience the authority of the Word.

    h. Be much in the faith of the promise that gives your soul an interest in God, Christ, and all good things.

    i. Remember the judgments of God that have or shall certainly overtake those professors who have either been downright hypocrites or else unwatchful Christians.

    j. Study the excellencies of the grace of fear and what profit it yields to those who have it.

    k. Remember what a world of privileges belong to those who fear.

    l. Be much in prayer for an abundance of the increase thereof.

    m. Devote yourself to it.

3. Ten hindrances given to the growth of the fear of God:

    a. A hard heart.

    b. A prayerless heart.

    c. A light and wanton heart .

    d. A covetous heart.

    e. An unbelieving heart.

D. *A word to hypocrites:*
1. Your condition is damnable.
2. You are naked before the eyes of God.
3. No obedience accepted by God where the heart is destitute of this grace of fear.
4. You must fear God first before trying to keep the commandments.
5. You forget to fear God.
6. None of the privileges of those that fear God belong to you.
7. You are not under the fatherly protection of God.
8. You are likely to have no other reward from God for your labor than that which the goats shall have.
9. God has not entrusted you with the least dram of His saving grace.
10. You are not true to God, nor man, nor your own soul.

Chapter 1

The Objects of and the Reasons for Fear

This exhortation is not only found here in Revelation 14:7, but is pressed in several other places of Scripture, and that with much vehemency, upon the children of men (see Ecclesiastes 12:13; 1 Peter 2:17). I shall not trouble you with a long preamble to the matter, nor shall I here meddle with the context, but shall immediately fall upon the words themselves and briefly treat the fear of God.

The text, you see, presents us with matter of the greatest moment, to wit, with God, and with the fear of Him.

First, it presents us with God, the true and living God, Maker of the worlds, and Upholder of all things by the word of His power. He is that incomprehensible Majesty in comparison to whom all nations are less than the drop of a bucket, or than a small dust in the balance. This is He who fills heaven and earth, and is everywhere present with the children of men, beholding the evil and the good; for He has set His eyes upon all their ways.

So considering that from the text we have presented to our souls the Lord God and Maker of us all, who also will be either our Savior or Judge, we are bound by both reason and duty to give the more earnest heed to the things that shall be spoken, and be the more careful to receive them and put them into practice; for, as I said, as they present us with

1

the mighty God, so they exhort us to the highest duty towards Him: to fear Him. I call it the highest duty because it is, as I may call it, not only a duty in itself, but, as it were, the salt that seasons every duty. For there is no duty performed by us that can by any means be accepted of God if it be not seasoned with godly fear. Wherefore the apostle says, "Let us have grace, whereby we may serve God acceptably with reverence and godly fear" (Hebrews 12:28). Of this fear I would discourse at this time; but because this word "fear" is used in different ways in Scripture, and because it may be profitable for us to see it in its various usages, I shall choose this method for the managing of my discourse, even to show you the nature of the word in its several uses, especially the chief ones.

First, by this word "fear" we are to understand God Himself, who is the object of our fear. Second, by this word "fear" we are to understand the Word of God, the rule and director of our fear.

I shall now speak of this word "fear" in the first of these two senses. It respects God Himself, who is the object of our fear; for the divine Majesty goes often under this very name Himself. Jacob called Him by this name when he and Laban were together on Mount Gilead, after Jacob had made his escape to his father's house: "Except the God of my father, the God of Abraham, and the Fear of Isaac, had been with me, surely thou hadst sent me away now empty" (Genesis 31:42). So again, a little later, when Jacob and Laban agreed to make a covenant of peace with each other: though Laban, after the jumbling way of the heathen by his oath, puts the true God and the false together, yet "Jacob sware by the Fear of his father Isaac" (Genesis 31:42, 53), that is, by the God of his father Isaac.

And, indeed, God may well be called "the Fear of His people," not only because they have by His grace made Him the object of their fear, but because of the dread and terrible majesty that is in Him. He is "a great and terrible God," and "with God is terrible majesty" (Nehemiah 1:5; 4:14; 9:32; Job 37:22).

Who knows the power of His anger? "The mountains quake at Him, and the hills melt, and the earth is burned at His presence, yea, the world, and all that dwell therein. Who can stand before His indignation? And who can abide in the fierceness of His anger? His fury is poured out like fire, and the rocks are thrown down by Him" (Nahum 1:5–6).

His people know Him, and have His dread upon them, by virtue whereof there is begotten and maintained in them that godly awe and reverence of His majesty which is agreeable to their profession of Him. "Let Him be your fear, and let Him be your dread" (Isaiah 8:13). Set His majesty before the eyes of your souls, and let His excellency make you afraid with godly fear.

The following things make God to be the fear of His people.

1. His presence is dreadful, and not only His presence in general, but His special, yea, His most comfortable and joyous presence. When God comes to bring a soul news of mercy and salvation, even that visit, that presence of God is fearful. When Jacob went from Beersheba towards Haran, he met with God in the way by a dream in which he saw a

ladder set up on the earth whose top reached to heaven. Now in this dream, from the top of this ladder, he saw the Lord, and heard Him speak unto him not threateningly, not as having His fury come up into his face, but in the most sweet and gracious manner, saluting him with promise of goodness after promise of goodness multiplied eight or nine times (Genesis 28:10–17). Yet, I say, when he awoke, all the grace that revealed itself in this heavenly vision to him could not keep him from the dread and fear of God's majesty. "And Jacob awoke out of his sleep, and he said, 'Surely the Lord is in this place and I knew it not.' And he was afraid, and said, 'How dreadful is this place! This is none other but the house of God, and this is the gate of heaven.' "

At another time, when Jacob had that memorable visit from God in which He gave him power as a prince to prevail with Him—yea, and gave him a name so that by his remembering it he might call God's favor the better to his mind—yet even then and there such dread of the majesty of God was upon him that he went away wondering that his life was preserved (Genesis 32:30). Man crumbles to dust at the presence of God, though He shows Himself to us in His robes of salvation.

We have read how dreadful and terrible even the presence of angels has been unto men, even when they have brought them good tidings from heaven (Judges 13:22; Matthew 28:5; Mark 16:5–6).

Now if angels, which are but creatures, are, through the glory that God has put upon them, so fearful and terrible in their appearance to men, how much more dreadful and terrible must God Himself be to us, who are but dust and ashes! When Daniel had the vision of his salvation sent him from heaven, "O Daniel," said the messenger, "a man greatly beloved"; yet behold, the dread and terror of the person speaking fell with such weight upon this good man's soul that he could neither stand nor bear up under it. He stood trembling and cried out, "O my lord, by the vision my sorrows are turned upon me, and I have retained no strength. For how can this servant of my lord talk with my lord? For as for me, straightway there remained no strength in me" (Daniel 10:16–17).

Take note: if the presence of God is not a dreadful and fearful thing even in His most gracious and merciful appearances, how much more so, then, when He shows Himself to us as one who dislikes our ways, as one who is offended with us for our sins! And there are three things that, in an eminent manner, make His presence dreadful to us.

(1) The first is God's own greatness and majesty; the discovery of this, or of Himself thus, even as no poor mortals are able to conceive of Him, is altogether unbearable. The man to whom God thus reveals Himself dies. "And when I saw Him," says John, "I fell at His feet as dead" (Revelation 1:17). It was this, therefore, that Job would have avoided in the day when he would have approached unto Him. "Let not Thy dread," says he, "make me afraid. Then call Thou, and I will answer; or let me speak, and answer Thou me" (Job 13:21–22). But why does Job speak to God after this manner? Why, it was from a sense that he had of the dreadful majesty of God, even the great and dreadful God who keeps

covenant with His people.

The presence of a king is dreadful to his subjects, even if he carries himself ever so condescendingly. If then there is so much glory and dread in the presence of a king, what fear and dread must there be in the presence of the eternal God!

(2) When God gives His presence to His people, that presence causes them to appear to themselves more as they are than at other times, by their usual light. "O my lord," said Daniel, "by the vision my sorrows are turned upon me"; and why was that but because, by the glory of that vision, he saw his own vileness more than at other times? So again: "I was left alone, and saw this great vision." And what follows? "And there remained no strength in me, for my comeliness was turned into corruption, and I retained no strength" (Daniel 10:8). By the presence of God, when we experience it, even our best things, our comeliness, our sanctity and righteousness, all immediately turn to corruption and polluted rags. The brightness of His glory dims them, as the clear light of the shining sun puts out the glory of the fire or candle, and covers them with the shadow of death.

You can also see the truth of this in the vision of the prophet Isaiah. "Woe is me," said he, "for I am undone, because I am a man of unclean lips, and I dwell in the midst of a people of unclean lips." Why, what was the matter? How did the prophet come to this sight? He adds, "For mine eyes have seen the King, the Lord of hosts" (Isaiah 6:5). But do you think that this outcry was caused by unbelief? No, nor was it begotten by slavish fear. It was Isaiah's vi-

sion of his Savior, with whom also he had previously
had communion. It was the glory of that God with
whom he had now to deal that turned, as was noted
before of Daniel, his comeliness into corruption,
and that gave him a yet greater sense of the dispro-
portion between his God and him, and so a greater
sight of his defiled and polluted nature.

(3) Add to this the revelation of God's goodness, and it must make His presence dreadful to us;
for when a poor, defiled creature shall see that this
great God has, notwithstanding His greatness,
goodness in His heart, and mercy to bestow upon
him, this makes His presence all the more dreadful.
They "shall fear the Lord and His goodness" (Hosea
3:5). The goodness as well as the greatness of God
begets in the heart of His elect an awful reverence of
His majesty. " 'Fear ye not Me?' saith the Lord. 'Will
ye not tremble at My presence?' " And then, to engage us in our souls to the duty, He adds one of His
wonderful mercies to the world for a motive. "Fear ye
not Me?" Why, who are you? I am He "who has
placed the sand for the bound of the sea by a perpetual decree, that it cannot pass it, and though the
waves thereof toss themselves, yet can they not prevail; though they roar, yet can they not pass over it"
(Jeremiah 5:22).

Also, when Job had God present with him, making manifest the goodness of His heart to him, what
did he say? How did he behave himself in God's
presence? "I have heard of Thee by the hearing of
the ear; but now mine eye seeth Thee. Wherefore I
abhor myself, and repent in dust and ashes" (Job
42:5–6).

And what do the tremblings, the tears, the break-
ings and shakings of heart mean that attend the
people of God, when in an eminent manner they receive the pronunciation of the forgiveness of sins
from His mouth, but that the dread of the majesty of
God is in their sight mixed therewith? God must appear like Himself and speak to the soul like Himself;
nor can the sinner, when under these glorious dis-
coveries of his Lord and Savior, keep out the beams
of His majesty from the eyes of his understanding. "I
will cleanse them," says He, "from all their iniquity,
whereby they have sinned against Me; and I will pardon all their iniquities whereby they have sinned,
and whereby they have transgressed against Me."
And what then? "And they shall fear and tremble for
all the goodness and for all the prosperity that I
procure unto them" (Jeremiah 33:8–9).

Alas, there is a company of poor, light, frothy
professors in the world who carry on under that notion which they call "the presence of God," but their
behavior is more like antics than sober, sensible
Christians; yea, more like fools than those who feel
the presence of God. They would not behave so in
the presence of a king, nor the lord of their land, if
they were receivers of mercy at his hand. They carry
on so even in their most eminent seasons, as if the
sense and sight of God, and His blessed grace to
their souls in Christ, had a tendency in them to
make men wanton. But, indeed, it is the most humbling and heartbreaking sight in the world; it is
fearful.

OBJECTION. But would you not have us rejoice
at sight and sense of the forgiveness of our sins?

ANSWER. Yes, but yet I would have you, and indeed you shall, when God shall tell you that your sins are pardoned, "rejoice with trembling" (Psalm 2:11). For then you will have solid and godly joy. At this time a joyful heart and wet eyes will go very well together, and it will be so more or less. For if God shall come to you, indeed, and visit you with the forgiveness of sins, that visit will remove the guilt, but increase the sense of your filth—and the sense of this, that God has forgiven a filthy sinner, will make you both rejoice and tremble. Oh, the blessed confusion that will then cover your face while you, even you, so vile a wretch, stand before God to receive at His hand your pardon, and so the first fruits of your eternal salvation! " 'That thou mayest remember, and be confounded, and never open thy mouth any more because of thy shame, when I am pacified toward thee for all that thou hast done,' saith the Lord God" (Ezekiel 16:63).

2. But as the presence of God is dreadful and fearful, so is the name of God; wherefore His name rightly goes under the same title: "that thou mayest fear this glorious and fearful name, THE LORD THY GOD" (Deuteronomy 28:58).

What is the name of God but that by which He is distinguished and known from all others? Names are to distinguish; so man is distinguished from beasts and angels from men; so heaven from earth and darkness from light—especially when, by the name, the nature of the thing is signified and expressed. And so it was originally, for then names expressed the nature of the thing so named. And therefore it is that the name of God is the object of our fear, because by His name His nature is expressed. "Holy and reverend is His name" (Psalm 111:9). And again: "The Lord, the Lord God, merciful and gracious, long-suffering, and abundant in goodness and truth, keeping mercy for thousands, forgiving iniquity and transgression and sin, and who will by no means clear the guilty" (Exodus 34: 6–7).

Also, what is intended by His names ("I AM," Jah, Jehovah, and several others) but that His nature, such as His power, wisdom, eternity, goodness, and omnipotence, might be expressed and declared? The name of God is, therefore, the object of a Christian's fear. David prayed to God, "Unite my heart to fear Thy name" (Psalm 86:11). Indeed, the name of God is a fearful name, and should always be reverenced by His people. Yea, His name is to be feared forever and ever, and that not only in His Church and among His saints, but even in the world and among the heathen. "So the heathen shall fear the name of the Lord, and all the kings of the earth Thy glory" (Psalm 102:15).

God tells us that His name is dreadful, and that He is pleased to see men afraid before His name (Malachi 2:5). Yea, one reason why He executes as many judgments upon men as He does is that others might see and fear His name. "So shall they fear the name of the Lord from the west, and His glory from the rising of the sun" (Isaiah 59:19). "I gave them to him for the fear wherewith he feared Me, and was afraid before My name" (Malachi 2:5).

The name of a king is a name of fear, and " 'I am a great King,' saith the Lord of hosts" (Malachi

1:14). The name of master is a name of fear: " 'And if
I be a Master, where is My fear?' saith the Lord of
hosts" (Malachi 1:6). Yea, rightly to fear the Lord is a
sign of a gracious heart. And again, "Unto you that
fear My name," says He, "shall the Sun of righteousness arise with healing in His wings." Yea, when
Christ comes to judge the world, He will give re-
wards to His servants the prophets, and to His saints,
and to those who fear His name, small and great
(Revelation 11:18).

Now, I say, since the name of God is that by
which His nature is expressed, and since He naturally is so glorious and incomprehensible, His name
should be the object of our fear, and we ought always
to have a reverential awe of God upon our hearts at
whatever time we think of or hear His name. But
most of all we should do so when we ourselves take
His holy and fearful name into our mouths, especially in a religious manner, that is, in preaching,
praying, or holy conference. I do not intend to say it
is lawful to make mention of His name in light and
vain discourses—for we ought always to speak of it
with reverence and godly fear—but I say this to put
Christians in mind that they should not show light-
ness of mind in religious duties or be vain in their
words when yet they are making mention of the
name of the Lord. "Let every one that nameth the
name of Christ depart from iniquity" (2 Timothy
2:19).

Make mention, then, of the name of the Lord at
all times with great dread of His majesty upon your
hearts, and in great soberness and truth. To do otherwise is to profane the name of the Lord and to

take His name in vain. "The Lord will not hold him
guiltless that taketh His name in vain" (Exodus
20:7). Yea, God says that He will cut off the man who
does it, so jealous is He of the honor due His name
(Leviticus 20:3).

This, therefore, shows you the dreadful state of
those who lightly, vainly, falsely, and profanely,
make use of this fearful name of God, either by their
blasphemous cursing and oaths or by their fraudu-
lent dealing with their neighbor. But how these
men, when they shall be judged, will escape devouring fire and everlasting burnings for their profan-
ing and blaspheming of the name of the Lord, it
behoves them quickly to consider.

3. But as the presence and name of God are
dreadful and fearful in the Church, so are His worship and service. I say, His worship, or the works of
service to which we are by Him enjoined while we
are in this world, are dreadful and fearful things.
David said, "But as for me, I will come into Thy
house in the multitude of Thy mercy, and in Thy
fear will I worship toward Thy holy temple" (Psalm
5:7). And again he says, "Serve the Lord with fear"
(Psalm 2:11).

To praise God is a part of His worship. But, said
Moses, "Who is like unto Thee, O LORD, among the
gods? Who is like Thee, glorious in holiness, fearful
in praises, doing wonders?" (Exodus 15:11). To rejoice before Him is a part of His worship; but David
bids us "rejoice with trembling" (Psalm 2:11).

Yea, the whole of our service to God, and every
part thereof, ought to be done by us with reverence
and godly fear (Hebrews 12:28). And, therefore, let

us, as Paul says again, "Cleanse ourselves from all filthiness of the flesh and spirit, perfecting holiness in the fear of God" (2 Corinthians 7:1).

That which makes the worship of God so fearful a thing is:

(1) It is the worship of God. All manner of service carries more or less dread and fear along with it according as the quality or condition of the person is to whom the worship and service are done. This is seen in the service of subjects to their princes, the service of servants to their lords, and the service of children to their parents. Divine worship, then, being due to God, and this God so great and dreadful in Himself and His name, His worship must, therefore, be a fearful thing.

(2) Besides, this glorious Majesty is Himself present to behold His worshippers in their worshipping Him. "Where two or three are gathered together in My name, there am I in the midst of them" (Matthew 18:20), that is, gathered together to worship Him. "I am there," says He. And so, again, He is said to walk in the midst of the seven golden candlesticks (Revelation 2:1), that is, in the churches, and that with a countenance like the sun, with a head and hair as white as wool, and with eyes like a flame of fire (Revelation 1:14–16). This puts dread and fear into His service; and, therefore, His servants should serve Him with fear.

(3) Above all things, God is jealous of His worship and service. In all the Ten Commandments, He tells us nothing of His being a jealous God but in the second, which respects His worship. Look to yourselves, therefore, both as to the matter and

manner of your worship. "For I the Lord thy God am a jealous God, visiting the iniquity of the fathers upon the children" (Exodus 20:5). This, therefore, also puts dread and fear into the worship and service of God.

(4) The judgments that God has sometimes executed upon men for their want of godly fear, while they have been in His worship and service, put fear and dread upon His holy appointments.

Nadab and Abihu were burned to death with fire from heaven because they attempted to offer false fire upon God's altar (Leviticus 10:1–3). And the reason rendered why they were so punished was that God will be sanctified in those who come near Him. To sanctify His name is to let Him be your dread and your fear, and to do nothing in His worship but what is well-pleasing to Him. But because these men had no grace to do this, therefore they died before the Lord.

Eli's sons, for want of this fear, when they ministered in the holy worship of God, were both slain in one day by the sword of the uncircumcised Philistines (1 Samuel 4:11).

Uzzah was smitten and died before the Lord for an unadvised touching of the ark, when the men forsook it (1 Chronicles 13:9–10).

Ananias and Sapphira, for telling a lie in the church when they were before God, were both struck dead before all the people, because they lacked the fear and dread of God's majesty, name, and service when they came before Him (Acts 5:1–10).

This, therefore, should teach us to conclude that, next to God's nature and name, His service, His instituted worship, is the most dreadful thing under heaven. His name is upon His ordinances. His eye is upon the worshippers, and His wrath and judgment are upon those who do not worship in His fear. For this cause some of those at Corinth were cut off by God Himself (1 Corinthians 11:30–32). On others He has turned His back, and will be with them no more.

This also rebukes three sorts of people:

1. Such as do not worship God at all. Be sure they have no reverence of His service, nor fear of His majesty before their eyes. Sinner, you do not come before the Lord to worship Him; you do not bow before the high God; neither do you worship Him in your closet, nor in the congregation of saints. The fury of the Lord and His indignation must, in a short time, be poured out upon you, and upon the families who do not call upon His name (Psalm 79:6; Jeremiah 10:25).

2. This rebukes such as count it enough to present their body in the place where God is worshipped, not minding with what heart or with what spirit they come there. Some come into the worship of God to sleep there; some come there to meet with their customers, and to get into the wicked fellowship of their vain companions; some come there to feed their lustful and adulterous eyes with the flattering beauty of their fellow sinners. Oh, what a sad account will these worshippers give when they shall account for all this, and be damned for it, because they did not come to worship the Lord with that fear of His name that they should have had when they presented themselves before Him!

3. This also rebukes those who do not care how,

where, or after what manner they worship God. I am speaking of those whose fear towards God is taught by the precepts of men. They are hypocrites; their worship also is vain, and a stench in the nostrils of God. Wherefore the Lord said, "Forasmuch as this people draw near Me with their mouth, and with their lips do honor Me, but have removed their heart far from Me, and their fear toward Me is taught by the precept of men, therefore, behold, I will proceed to do a marvelous work among this people, even a marvelous work and a wonder; for the wisdom of their wise men shall perish, and the understanding of their prudent men shall be hid" (Isaiah 29:13–14).

Thus I conclude this first point, namely that God is called our dread and fear.

Chapter 2

The Rule of Fear, and Its Various Kinds

I shall now come to the second point, the rule and directory of our fear. This word "fear" is also taken to mean the Word of God, the written Word of God; for that also is and ought to be the rule and directory of our fear. So David calls it: "The fear of the Lord is clean, enduring forever" (Psalm 19:9). The fear of the Lord here is the Word of the Lord, the written Word, for that which he calls in this place "the fear of the Lord" he also refers to as the law, statutes, commandments, and judgments of God. "The law of the Lord is perfect, converting the soul; the testimony of the Lord is sure, making wise the simple. The statutes of the Lord are right, rejoicing the heart; the commandment of the Lord is pure, enlightening the eyes. The fear of the Lord is clean, enduring forever; the judgments of the Lord are true and righteous altogether" (verses 7–9). All these words have respect to the same thing, the Word of God, jointly designing the glory of it.

"The fear of the Lord is clean, enduring forever." This written Word is, therefore, the object of a Christian's fear. This is that also which David intended when he said, "Come, ye children, hearken unto me. I will teach you the fear of the Lord" (Psalm 34:11). "I will teach you the fear," that is, I will teach you the commandments, statutes, and judgments of the Lord, even as Moses commanded the children of

17

Israel: "Thou shalt teach them diligently unto thy children, and shalt talk of them when thou sittest in thine house, and when thou walkest by the way, and when thou liest down, and when thou risest up" (Deuteronomy 6:7).

That Scripture also in Isaiah intends the same where the Father says that the Son shall be "of quick understanding in the fear of the Lord," that He may "smite the earth with the rod of His mouth" (Isaiah 11:3–4). This rod in the text is none other than the fear, the Word of the Lord; for He was to be of a quick understanding in it that He might smite, that is, execute it according to the will of His Father upon and among the children of men.

Now this, as I said, is called "the fear of the Lord" because it is the rule and directory of our fear. For we know not how to fear the Lord in a saving way without its guidance and direction. As it is said of the priest who was sent back from the captivity to Samaria to teach the people to fear the Lord, so it is said concerning the written Word: it is given to us, and left among us, that we may read therein all the days of our life and learn to fear the Lord (see Deuteronomy 6:1–24; 10:12; 17:19).

And here it is that trembling at the Word of God is not only taken notice of even by God Himself, but counted as laudable and praiseworthy, as is evident in the case of Josiah (2 Chronicles 34:26–27).

Such also are the approved of God, let them be condemned by whomsoever they may. "Hear the Word of the Lord, ye that tremble at His Word. Your brethren that hated you, that cast you out for My name's sake, said, 'Let the Lord be glorified'; but He shall appear to your joy, and they shall be ashamed" (Isaiah 66:5).

Further, such shall be looked to by God Himself, cared for and watched over, so that no distress, temptation, or affliction may overcome and destroy them. "To this man will I look," says God, "even to him that is poor and of a contrite spirit, and trembleth at My Word" (Isaiah 66:2). It is the same in substance as that other passage from the same prophet: "For thus saith the high and lofty One that inhabiteth eternity, whose name is Holy: 'I dwell in the high and holy place, with him also that is of a contrite and humble spirit, to revive the spirit of the humble, and to revive the heart of the contrite ones' " (Isaiah 57:15). Yea, the way to escape dangers foretold is to hearken to, understand, and fear the Word of God. "He that feared the Word of the Lord among the servants of Pharaoh made his servants and his cattle flee into the houses; and he that regarded not the Word of the Lord left his servants and his cattle in the field"; and they were destroyed by the hail (Exodus 9:20–25).

If at any time the sins of a nation or church are discovered and bewailed, it is by those who know and tremble at the Word of God. When Ezra heard of the wickedness of his brothers, and had a desire to humble himself before God for the same, who were those who assisted him in that matter but those who trembled at the Word of God? "Then," says he, "were assembled unto me everyone that trembled at the words of the God of Israel, because of the transgression of those that had been carried away" (Ezra 9:4).

Those also who tremble at the Word are best able to give counsel in the matters of God, for their judgment is best suited with His mind and will. "Now therefore," said Shechaniah, "let us make a covenant with our God to put away all the [foreign] wives, and such as are born of them, according to the counsel of my lord, and of those that tremble at the commandment of our God; and let it be done according to the law" (Ezra 10:3).

Now something of the dread and terror of the Word lies in these things:

1. As I have already hinted from the Author of them, they are the words of God. Therefore you have Moses and the prophets, when they come to deliver their message to the people, still saying, "Hear the word of the Lord," "Thus says the Lord," and the like. So when Ezekiel was sent to the house of Israel in their state of religion, he was bid to say unto them, "Thus saith the Lord God" (Ezekiel 2:4; 3:11).

This is the honor and majesty, then, that God has put upon His written Word; and thus He has done that we might make it the rule and directory of our fear, and that we might stand in awe of and tremble at it. When Habakkuk heard the word of the Lord, his belly trembled and rottenness entered into his bones. "I trembled in myself that I might rest in the day of trouble" (Habakkuk 3:16). The word of a king is as the roaring of a lion; where the word of a king is there is power (Ecclesiastes 8:4). What is it, then, when the great God shall roar out of Zion and utter His voice from Jerusalem, whose voice shakes not only earth, but also heaven? How does holy David set it forth? "The voice of the Lord is powerful;

the voice of the Lord is full of majesty" (Psalm 29:4)!

2. It is a Word that is fearful, and may well be called "the fear of the Lord," because of the subject matter of it, namely the state of sinners in another world; for that is the topic unto which the whole Bible bends itself, either more immediately or more mediately. All its doctrines, counsels, encouragements, threatenings, and judgments relate in one way or another upon us to the next world, which will be our last state because it will be to us an eternal state. This Word, this law, these judgments are that by which we shall be disposed of. "The word that I have spoken," said Christ, "the same shall judge him in the last day" (John 12:48). Now if we consider that our next state must be eternal, either eternal glory or eternal fire, and that this eternal glory or eternal fire must be our portion according as the words of God, revealed in the Holy Scriptures, shall determine, who will not but conclude that, therefore, the words of God are those at which we should tremble, and those by which we should have our fear of God guided and directed? For by them we are taught how to please Him in everything.

3. It is to be called a fearful Word because of the truth and faithfulness of it. "The Scripture cannot be broken" (John 10:35). Hence it is called "the Scripture of truth" (Daniel 10:21), "the true sayings of God" (Revelation 19:9), and also the fear of the Lord, for every jot and tittle thereof is forever settled in heaven, and stands more steadfast than does the world. "Heaven and earth," said Christ, "shall pass away, but My Word shall not pass away" (Matthew 24:35). Those therefore who are favored by the Word

of God are favored indeed, and that with the favor that no man can turn away; but those who, by the word of the Scriptures, are condemned, no man can justify and set right in the sight of God. Therefore, what is bound by the text is bound, and what is released by the text is released; also, the bond and release are unalterable. This therefore calls upon God's people to stand more in fear of the Word of God than of all the terrors of the world.

There lacks even in the hearts of God's people a greater reverence of the Word of God than to this day appears among us; and that want of reverence for the Word is the ground of all the disorders that are in the heart, life, conversation, and in Christian communion. Besides, the want of reverence of the Word lays men open to the fearful displeasure of God. "Whoso despiseth the Word shall be destroyed; but he that feareth the commandment shall be rewarded" (Proverbs 13:13).

All transgression begins at wandering from the Word of God; but, on the other side, David says, "Concerning the works of men, by the word of Thy lips I have kept me from the paths of the destroyer" (Psalm 17:4). Therefore Solomon says, "My son, attend to my words; incline thine ear unto my sayings. Let them not depart from thine eyes; keep them in the midst of thine heart. For they are life unto those that find them, and health to all their flesh" (Proverbs 4:20–22).

Now, if indeed you would reverence the Word of the Lord and make it your rule and directory in all things, believe that the Word is the fear of the Lord—the Word that stands fast forever, without and against which God will do nothing either in saving or condemning the souls of sinners.

But to conclude this, know that those who have no due regard for the Word of the Lord, and who make it not their dread and their fear (but the rule of their life is the lusts of their flesh, the desire of their eyes, and the pride of life), are sorely rebuked by this doctrine, and are counted as the fools of the world. "Lo, they have rejected the word of the Lord; and what wisdom is in them?" (Jeremiah 8:9). That there are such people is evident not only by their irregular lives, but by the manifest testimony of the Word. "As for the word," said they to Jeremiah, "that thou hast spoken unto us in the name of the Lord, we will not hearken unto thee. But we will certainly do whatsoever thing goeth out of our own mouth" (Jeremiah 44:16–17).

Was this only the temper of wicked men then? Is not the same spirit of rebellion among us in our day? Doubtless there is, for there is no new thing: "The thing that hath been, it is that which shall be; and that which is done is that which shall be done, and there is no new thing under the sun" (Ecclesiastes 1:9).

Therefore, as it was then, so it is with many in this day. As for the Word of the Lord, it is nothing at all to them; their lusts, and whatever proceeds out of their own mouths, that they will do; that they will follow. Now such will certainly perish in their rebellion, for this is as the sin of witchcraft; it was the sin of Korah and his company, and that which brought upon them such heavy judgments; yea, and they are made a sign so that you do not do as they, for they perished (because they rejected the Word, the fear of the Lord) from among the congregation of the Lord, and they became a sign. The Word which you despise still abides to pronounce its woe and judgment upon you; and unless God will save you with the breath of His Word, you cannot ever see His face with comfort.

Are the words of God called by the name of "the fear of the Lord"? Are they so dreadful in their receipt and sentence? Then this rebukes those who esteem the world and things of men more than the words of God, as those do who are drawn from their respect of and obedience to the Word of God by the pleasures or threats of men.

There are some who verily will acknowledge the authority of the Word, yet will not stoop their souls thereto. Such, whatever they think of themselves, are judged by Christ to be ashamed of the Word—wherefore their estate is as damnable as the other. "Whosoever," says He, "shall be ashamed of Me and of My words in this adulterous and sinful generation, of him also shall the Son of Man be ashamed when He cometh in the glory of His Father with the holy angels" (Mark 8:38).

4. And if these things are so, what will become of those who mock at and professedly condemn the words of God, making them as a ridiculous thing which is not to be regarded? Shall they prosper who do such things? From the premises it is concluded that their judgment will not slumber for a long time, and when it comes it will devour them without remedy (see 2 Chronicles 36:15–16).

If God, I say, has put such reverence upon His

Word as to call it "the fear of the Lord," what will become of those who do what they can to overthrow its authority by denying it to be His Word, and by raising cavils against its authority? Such stumble indeed at the Word, being appointed thereunto; but it shall judge them in the last day (1 Peter 2:8; John 12:48). But so much for this.

Having thus spoken of the object and rule of our fear, I come now to speak of fear as a grace of the Spirit of God in the hearts of His people. But before I do that, I shall show you that there are divers sorts of fear besides. For man, being a reasonable creature, and having even by nature a certain knowledge of God, has also naturally a kind of fear of God at times, which, although it be not that which is intended in the text, yet ought to be spoken to so that that which is not right may be distinguished from that which is.

I will speak of several sorts of the fear of God in the hearts of the children of men, besides that fear of God which is intended in the text, and which accompanies eternal life. I shall here make mention of three of them:

1. There is a fear of God which flows from the light of nature.

2. There is a fear of God which flows from some of His dispensations to men, which yet is neither universal nor saving.

3. There is a fear of God in the hearts of some men which is good and godly, but does not forever abide so.

I wish to speak a little to all these before I come

to speak of fear as a grace of God in the hearts of His children.

1. There is a fear of God which flows from the light of nature.

People may be said to do things in the fear of God when they act one towards another in things reasonable and honest between man and man, not doing that to others that they would not have done to themselves. This is that fear of God which Abraham thought the Philistines had destroyed in themselves, when he said of his wife to Abimelech, "She is my sister." For when Abimelech asked Abraham why he said of his wife, "She is my sister," he replied, saying, "I thought, 'Surely the fear of God is not in this place, and they will slay me for my wife's sake' " (Genesis 20:11). In other words, he thought, verily, that in this place men had stifled and choked that light of nature which is in them, at least so far as not to suffer it to put them in fear, when their lusts were powerful in them to accomplish their ends on the object that was present before them. But this I will pass by and come to the second thing:

2. There is a fear of God which flows from some of His dispensations to men, which yet is neither universal nor saving. This fear, when opposed to that which is saving, may be called an ungodly fear of God. I shall describe it by several particulars:

(1) There is a fear of God that causes a continual begrudging, discontent and heart-risings against God when a person is under the hand of God—that is, when the dread of God in His coming upon men to deal with them for their sins is appre-

hended by them, and yet by this dispensation they have no change of heart to submit to Him thereunder.

Sinners under this dispensation cannot shake God out of their mind, nor yet graciously tremble before Him, but through the unsanctified frame that they now are in they are afraid with ungodly fear, and so in their minds are against Him.

This fear oftentimes took hold of the children of Israel when they were in the wilderness in their journey to the promised land; still they feared that God in this place would destroy them, but not with that fear that made them willing to submit because of their sins to the judgment which they feared, but with that fear which made them oppose God.

This fear showed itself in them even at the beginning of their journey, and was rebuked by Moses at the Red Sea. But it was not there, nor yet at any other place, so subdued but that it would rise again in them at times to the dishonor of God, and make them anew guilty of sin before Him (see Exodus 14:11–12; Numbers 14:1–10).

This fear is that which God said He would send before them in the day of Joshua, a fear that would possess the inhabitants of the land, a fear that would arise for that faintness of heart by which they would be swallowed up at their apprehending Joshua in his approaches towards them to destroy them. "I will send My fear before thee, and will destroy all the people to whom thou shalt come, and I will make all thine enemies turn their backs unto thee" (Exodus 23:27). "This day," said God, "will I begin to put the dread of thee and the fear of thee upon the nations that are under the whole heavens, who shall hear report of thee, and shall tremble, and be in anguish because of thee" (Deuteronomy 2:25).

Now this fear is also, as you see here, called "anguish," and in another place "a hornet"; for it and the soul that it falls upon greet each other as boys and bees do. The hornet puts men in fear, not so as to bring the heart into a sweet compliance with his terror, but so as to stir up the spirit into acts of opposition and resistance; yet withal they flee before it. "I will send hornets before thee, which shall drive out the Hivite, the Canaanite, and the Hittite from before thee" (Exodus 23:28).

Now as for this fear, whether it is wrought by a misapprehension of the judgments of God, as in the Israelites, or otherwise, as in the Canaanites, yet ungodliness is the effect thereof; and therefore I call it an ungodly fear of God, for it stirs up murmurings, discontents, and heart-risings against God, while He, with His dispensations, is dealing with them.

(2) There is a fear of God that drives a man away from God. I speak not now of the atheist, nor of the pleasurable sinner, nor yet of that fear of which I just now spoke; but I speak now of such who, through a sense of sin and of God's justice, flee from Him by a slavish, ungodly fear. This ungodly fear was that which possessed Adam's heart in the day that he ate of the tree concerning which the Lord had said unto him, "In the day that thou eatest thereof thou shalt surely die" (Genesis 2:17). For then was he possessed with such a fear of God as made him seek to hide himself from His presence. "I heard," said he, "Thy voice in the garden, and I

was afraid, because I was naked; and I hid myself"
(Genesis 3:10). Note that he had a fear of God, but it
was not godly. It was not that which made him afterwards submit himself unto Him; for that would
have kept him from departing from Him, or else
would have brought him to God again with a bowed,
broken, and contrite spirit. But this fear, as the rest
of his sin, managed his departing from his God, and
pursued him to provoke him still so to do. By it he
kept himself from God; by it his whole man was carried away from Him. I call it ungodly fear because it
begat in him ungodly apprehensions of his Maker;
because it confined Adam's conscience to the sense
of justice only, and consequently to despair.

The same fear also possessed the children of
Israel when they heard the law delivered to them
from Mount Sinai. This is evident, for it made them
so that they could neither abide God's presence nor
hear His word. It drove them back from the mountain. It made them, says the apostle to the Hebrews,
so that "they could not endure that which was commanded" (Hebrews 12:20). Wherefore this fear
Moses rebukes, and forbids their giving way thereto.
"Fear not," said he; but had that fear been godly, he
would have encouraged it, not forbidden and rebuked it as he did. "Fear not," said he, "for God is
come to prove you, and that His fear may be before
your faces" (Exodus 20:20). Therefore, that fear
which already had taken possession of them was not
the fear of God, but a fear that was of Satan, of their
own misjudging hearts, and so a fear that was ungodly. Mark it, here are two fears: a fear forbidden
and a fear commended—a fear forbidden because it

engendered their hearts to bondage, and to ungodly thoughts of God and of His word; it made them that they could not desire to "hear God speak to them anymore" (verse 19).

Many also at this day are possessed with this ungodly fear; and you may know them by this: they cannot abide conviction for sin. And if at any time the word of the law, by the preaching of the Word, comes near them, they will not abide that preacher, nor such kinds of sermons any more. They are, as they deem, best at ease when furthest off from God and the power of His Word. The Word preached brings God nearer to them than they desire He should come because, whenever God comes near, their sins are manifest by Him, and so is the judgment that to them is due. Now, these not having faith in the mercy of God through Christ, nor that grace that tends to bring them to Him, they cannot but think of God amiss; and their so thinking of Him makes them say unto God, "Depart from us; for we desire not the knowledge of Thy ways" (Job 21:14). Wherefore their wrong thoughts of God beget in them this ungodly fear; and, again, this ungodly fear maintains in them the continuance of these wrong and unworthy thoughts of God. And therefore, through that devilish service wherewith they strengthen one another, the sinner, unless a miracle of grace prevents him, is drowned in destruction and perdition.

It was this ungodly fear of God that carried Cain from the presence of God into the land of Nod, and that put him there upon any carnal, worldly business, if perhaps he might in so doing stifle convic-

tions of the majesty and justice of God against his
sin, and so live the rest of his vain life in the more
sinful security and fleshly ease.

This ungodly fear is that also which Samuel perceived, at the people's apprehension of their sin, to
begin to get hold of their hearts; wherefore he, as
Moses before him, quickly forbade their entertaining of it. "Fear not," said he; "ye have done all this
wickedness, yet turn not aside from following the
Lord" (1 Samuel 12:20). For to turn them aside from
following Him was the natural tendency of this fear.
But fear not, said he, that is, with that fear that tends
to turn you aside.

Now, I say, the matter that this fear worked upon
(as in Adam and the Israelites, mentioned before)
was their sin. You have sinned, said Samuel, that is
true, yet turn not aside; yet fear not with that fear
that would make you so do. Note by the way, sinner,
that when the greatness of your sins, being apprehended by you, shall work in you that fear of God as
shall incline your heart to flee from Him, you are
possessed with a fear of God that is ungodly, yea, so
ungodly that not one of your sins (as for heinous-
ness) may be compared therewith, as might be made
manifest in many particulars. But Samuel, having
rebuked this fear, presently set before the people
another, to wit, the true fear of God. "Fear the Lord,"
said he, "and serve Him in truth with all your heart"
(verse 24). And he gave them this encouragement so
to do: "for the Lord will not forsake His people"
(verse 22).

This ungodly fear is that which you read of in
many other places; and God's people should shun it

as they would shun the devil, because its natural tendency is to forward the destruction of the soul of which it has taken possession.

(3) There is a fear of God which, although it does not have in it that power to make men flee from God's presence, yet is ungodly because, even while they are in the outward way of God's ordinances, their hearts are quite discouraged by it from attempting to exercise themselves in the power of religion.

Of this sort are those who dare not cast off the hearing, reading, and discoursing of the Word as others do; no, nor the assembly of God's children for the exercise of other religious duties, for their conscience is convinced this is the way and worship of God. Yet their heart is, by this ungodly fear, kept from a powerful, gracious falling in with God. This fear takes away their heart from all holy and godly prayer in private, and from all holy and godly zeal for His name in public; and there are many professing Christians whose hearts are possessed with this ungodly fear of God. They are the ones represented by the slothful servant. He was a servant, a servant among the servants of God, and had gifts and abilities given him therewith to serve Christ as well as his fellow men; yea, and he was commanded as well as the rest to occupy till his master came. But what did he do? Why, he took his talent, the gift that he was to lay out for his master's profit, and put it in a napkin; he dug a hole in the earth, hid his lord's money, and lay around in a lazy manner all his days, not out of, but in his lord's vineyard—for the lord came among the servants also at last. By this it is manifest that he had not cast off his profession, but was slothful and negligent while he was in it. But what was it that made him so slothful? What was it that took away his heart while he was in the way, and that discouraged him from falling in with the power and holy practice of religion according to the talent he received? Why, it was this: he gave way to an ungodly fear of God, and that took away his heart from the power of religious duties. "Lord," said he, "behold, here is your pound, which I have kept laid up in a napkin, for I feared you." Why, does the fear of God make a man idle and slothful? No, no, not if it is right and godly. This fear was, therefore, evil fear; it was that ungodly fear of God of which I have here been speaking. "For I fear Thee," or as Matthew has it, "for I was afraid." Afraid of what? Afraid that Christ was a hard man, reaping where He sowed not, and gathering where He had not strewn. His fear, being ungodly, made him apprehend Christ contrary to the goodness of His nature, and so took away his heart from all endeavors to be doing that which was pleasing in His sight (Luke 19:20–26; Matthew 25:24–30).

And thus do all those who retain the name and show of religion, but neglect the power and godly practice of it. These will live like dogs and swine in the house. They do not pray; they do not watch their hearts; they do not pull their hands out of their bosoms to work; they do not strive against their lusts, nor will they ever resist unto blood, striving against sin; they will not take up their cross or improve what they have to God's glory.

Let all men, therefore, take heed of this ungodly

fear and shun it, for it will make them afraid where no fear is. It will tell them that there is a lion in the street, the most unlikely place in the world for such a beast to be; it will put a mask upon the face of God, most dreadful and fearful to behold, and then quite discourage the soul as to His service. So it served the slothful servant, and so it will serve you, poor sinner, if you entertain it and give way thereto.

(4) This ungodly fear of God shows itself also in this: it will not suffer the soul that is governed thereby to trust Christ alone for justification of life, but will bend the powers of the soul to trust partly in the works of the law. Many of the Jews were, in the time of Christ and His apostles, possessed with this ungodly fear of God. They were not like the slothful servant, receiving a talent and hiding it in the earth in a napkin; but they were an industrious people "which followed after the law of righteousness" (Romans 9:31). They had a zeal for God and for the religion of their fathers; how, then, did they come to miscarry? Why, their fear of God was ungodly; it would not suffer them wholly to trust to the righteousness of faith, which is the imputed righteousness of Christ. They followed after the law of righteousness, but did not attain to the law of righteousness. "Wherefore? Because they sought it not by faith, but as if it were by the works of the law" (Romans 9:32). What was it that made them join their works of the law with Christ but their unbelief, whose foundation was ignorance and fear? They were afraid to venture all in one bottom; they thought two strings to one bow would be best, and thus between two stools they came to the ground.

And hence fearing and doubting are put together as being the cause one of another; yea, they are put oftentimes one for the other. Thus ungodly fear is put for unbelief: "Be not afraid, only believe" (Mark 5:36). And therefore he who is ruled by and carried away with this fear is coupled with the unbeliever who is thrust out from the holy city among the dogs. "But the fearful, the unbelievers, the murderers" are without (Revelation 21:8). The fearful and unbelieving, you see, are put together; for, indeed, fear, that is, this ungodly fear, is the ground of unbelief. Or, if you will, unbelief is the ground of this fear. But I stand not upon nice distinctions. This ungodly fear has a great hand in keeping the soul from trusting Christ's righteousness alone for justification of life.

(5) This ungodly fear of God is that which will make men add to the revealed will of God—adding their own inventions and their own performances of them as a means to pacify the anger of God. The truth is, where this ungodly fear reigns there is no end of law and duty. When those people of whom you read in 2 Kings 17:26 were destroyed by the lions because they had set up idolatry in the land of Israel, they sent for a priest from Babylon who might teach them the manner of the god of the land; but, behold, when they knew it, being taught by the priest, yet their fear would not suffer them to be content with that worship only. "They feared the Lord, and served their own gods" (verse 33). And, again, "so these nations feared the Lord, and served their graven images" (verse 41). It was this fear also that made the Pharisees invent so many traditions, such as washing cups, pots, brazen vessels and ta-

bles, with an abundance of other like things (Mark 7:4). None knows the many dangers that an ungodly fear of God will drive a man into. How has it racked and tortured the papists for hundreds of years together! For what else is the cause, at least in the most simple and harmless of them, of their penances, such as creeping to the cross, going barefoot on a pilgrimage, whipping themselves, wearing sackcloth, saying so many *paternosters*, so many *ave marias*, making so many confessions to the priest, giving so much money for pardons, and abundance of others, but this ungodly fear of God? For could they be brought to believe this doctrine, that Christ "was delivered for our offenses, and was raised again for our justification" (Romans 4:25), and to apply it by faith with godly boldness to their own souls, this fear would vanish, and so, consequently, would all those things with which they so needlessly and unprofitably afflict themselves, which are very offensive to God, and grieve His people.

Therefore, gentle reader, although my text does indeed bid that you should fear God, yet it does not include or accept *any* fear of God. For there is, as you see, a fear of God that is ungodly, and that is to be shunned as other sins. Wherefore your wisdom and your care should be to see and prove your fear to be godly, which shall be the next thing that I shall take in hand.

3. There is a fear of God in the hearts of some men that is good and godly, yet does not forever abide so. Or you may take it thus: there is a fear of God that is godly for only a time.

In opening this to you:

I shall show you what this fear is.

I shall show you by whom or by what this fear is wrought in the heart.

I shall show you what this fear does in the soul.

First, this fear is an effect of sound awakenings by the word of wrath, which begets in the soul a sense of its right to eternal damnation; for this fear is not in every sinner. He who is blinded by the devil, and who is not able to see that his state is damnable, has not this fear in his heart. But he who is under the powerful workings of the word of wrath, as God's elect are at first conversion, has this godly fear in his heart. That is, he fears that that damnation which by the justice of God is due unto him will come upon him because he has broken His holy law. This is the fear that made the three thousand cry out, "Men and brethren, what shall we do?" (Acts 2:37), and that made the jailer cry out, and that with great trembling of soul, "Sirs, what must I do to be saved?" (Acts 16:30).

The method of God is to kill and then make alive, to smite and then heal. When the commandment came to Paul, sin revived and he died; and that law which was ordained to life he found to be unto death (Romans 7:9–10). That is, it passed a sentence of death upon him for his sins and slew his conscience with that sentence. Therefore, from the time that he heard that word, "Why dost thou persecute me?" (which is as if He had said, "Why dost thou commit murder?"), he lay under the sentence of condemnation by the law, and under this fear of that sentence in his conscience. He lay, I say, under it until Ananias came to comfort him, and to preach unto him the forgiveness of sins (Acts 9:17).

The fear, therefore, that I am calling "godly" is
that fear which is properly called the fear of eternal
damnation for sin; and this fear, at first awakening,
is good and godly because it rises in the soul from a
true sense of its very state. Its state by nature is
damnable because it is sinful, and because the person is not one who yet believes in Christ for remis-
sion of sins. "He that believeth not shall be
damned" (Mark 16:16). "He that believeth not is
condemned already," and "the wrath of God abideth
on him" (John 3:18, 36). When the sinner at first begins to see this, he justly fears it; I say, he fears it
justly, and therefore in a godly way, because by this
fear he subscribes to the sentence that has gone out
against him for sin.

*Second, this fear is wrought in the heart by the Spirit of
God, working there at first as a Spirit of bondage to purposely
put us in fear.* This Paul teaches in Romans 8:15, saying, "Ye have not received the spirit of bondage
again to fear." He does not say, "Ye have not received
the Spirit of bondage," for they had received that,
and it put them in fear, which was at their first conversion, as by the instances mentioned before is
manifest. All that he says is that they had not received it again—that is, after the Spirit, as a Spirit of
adoption has come; for then, it comes no more as a
spirit of bondage.

It is then the Spirit of God, even the Holy Ghost,
who convinces us of sin, and so of our damnable
state because of sin (John 16:8–9). For it cannot be
that the Spirit of God should convince us of sin but
it must also show us that our state is damnable be-

cause of it, especially if it so convinces us before we believe. And that is what our Lord intended in that passage when He spoke of being convicted "of sin" (and so of their damnable state by sin) "because they believe not on Me." Therefore the Spirit of God, when He works in the heart as a Spirit of bondage, does it by working in us by the law. "For by the law is the knowledge of sin" (Romans 3:20). And in His working, He is properly called "a Spirit of bondage":

(1) Because by the law He shows us that, indeed, we are in bondage to the law, the devil, death, and damnation; for this is our proper state by nature, though we see it not until the Spirit of God comes to reveal our state of bondage unto our own senses by revealing to us our sins by the law.

(2) He is called in His working "the Spirit of bondage" because He here also holds us, to wit, in this sight and sense of our state of bondage so long as is meet we should be so held, which to some of the saints is a longer and to some a shorter time. Paul was held in it three days and three nights, but the jailer and the three thousand, so far as can be gathered, not more than an hour. But some in these later times are so held for days and months, if not years.

But I say, let the time be longer or shorter, it is the Spirit of God who holds him under His yoke; and it is good that a man should be held under it for this time. "It is good for a man that he bear the yoke in his youth" (Lamentations 3:27), that is, at his first awakening, as long as seems good to this Holy Spirit to work in this manner by the law.

Now, as I said, the sinner at first is by the Spirit of

God held in this bondage; that is, he has such a discovery of his sin, and of his damnation for sin, made to him, and also is held so fast under the sense thereof, that it is not in the power of any man, nor yet of the very angels in heaven, to release him, or set him free, until the Holy Spirit changes His ministration, and comes in the sweet and peaceable tidings of salvation by Christ in the gospel, to his poor, dejected, and afflicted conscience.

Third, I will show you what this fear does in the soul.

Although this godly fear is not to last always with us, yet it greatly differs from that which is wholly ungodly of itself, both because of the author and the effects of it. Of the author I have told you before; I now shall tell you what it does.

(1) This fear makes a man judge himself for sin, and fall down before God with a broken heart under this judgment. This is pleasing to God because the sinner, by so doing, justifies God in his saying and clears Him in his judgment.

(2) As this fear makes a man judge and cast himself down at God's footstool, so it makes him regret and bewail his misery before Him, which is also well-pleasing in His sight. "I have surely heard Ephraim bemoaning himself thus: 'Thou hast chastised me, and I was chastised, as a bullock unaccustomed to the yoke; turn Thou me, and I shall be turned; for Thou art the Lord my God. Surely after I was turned, I repented; and after I was instructed I smote upon my thigh. I was ashamed, yea, even confounded, because I did bear the reproach of my youth' " (Jeremiah 31:18–19).

(3) This fear makes a man lie at God's foot-

stool and puts his mouth in the dust, if perchance there may be hope. This also is well-pleasing to God because now the sinner is as nothing, and in his own eyes less than nothing, as to any good or merit. "He sitteth alone and keepeth silence, because He hath borne it upon him. He putteth his mouth in the dust; if so be there may be hope" (Lamentations 3:28–29).

(4) This fear makes a man cry to God for mercy, and that in a most humble manner. Now he sensibly cries; now he dejectedly cries; now he feels and cries; now he smarts and cries out, "God be merciful to me, a sinner" (Luke 18:13).

(5) This fear makes a man so that he cannot accept for support and succor what others who are destitute thereof will take up and be contented with. This man must be washed by God Himself, and cleansed from his sin by God Himself (Psalm 51).

(6) Therefore, this fear does not go away until the Spirit of God changes His ministration as to this particular, in ceasing to work by the law as before, and coming to the soul with the sweet word of promise of life and salvation by Jesus Christ.

Thus far this fear is godly—that is, until Christ by the Spirit in the gospel is revealed and made over unto us and no longer. Thus far this fear is godly, and the reason it is godly is that the groundwork of it is good. I told you before what this fear is; namely it is the fear of damnation. Now, the ground for this fear is good, as is manifest by these particulars:

The soul fears damnation, and that rightly, because it is in its sins.

The soul fears damnation rightly because it has

no faith in Christ, but is at present under the law.

The soul fears damnation rightly because by sin, by the law, and for lack of faith the wrath of God abides on it.

But now although thus far this fear of God is good and godly, yet after Christ, by the Spirit in the word of the gospel, is revealed to us, and we are brought to accept Him as so revealed and offered to us by a true and living faith—this fear of damnation is no longer good, but ungodly. Nor does the Spirit of God ever work it in us again. "For ye have not received the Spirit of bondage again to fear," that is to say, to fear damnation, "but ye have received the Spirit of adoption, whereby we cry, 'Abba, Father' " (Romans 8:15).

But I would not be misunderstood when I say that this fear is no longer godly. I do not mean with reference to the essence and habit of it—for I believe it is the same in the seed, which shall afterwards grow up to a higher degree, and into a more sweet and gospel current, and manner of working—but I mean with reference to this act of fearing damnation. I say, it shall never by the Spirit be led to that work; it shall never bring forth that fruit more.

And my reasons are, first, that the soul, by closing through the promise, by the Spirit, with Jesus Christ, is removed off the foundation upon which it stood when it justly feared damnation. It has now received forgiveness of sin; it is now no more under the law, but in Jesus Christ by faith. Therefore there is now no condemnation for it (Romans 8:1). The groundwork being taken away, the Spirit works that fear no more.

Second, He cannot, after He has come to the soul as a Spirit of adoption, come again as a Spirit of bondage to put the soul into its first fear, to wit, a fear of eternal damnation, because He cannot say and unsay, do and undo. As a Spirit of adoption He told me that my sins were forgiven me, that I was included in the covenant of grace, that God was my Father through Christ, that I was under the promise of salvation, and that this calling and gift of God to me is permanent and without repentance. And do you think that after He has told me this, and sealed the truth of it to my precious soul, He will come to me and tell me that I am yet in my sins, under the curse of the law and the eternal wrath of God? No, no, the word of the gospel is not "yea, yea" and then "nay, nay." It is only "yea, and amen"; it is so as God is true (2 Corinthians 1:17, 20).

Third, the state, therefore, of the sinner being changed, and that too by the Spirit's changing His dispensation—ceasing to be now a Spirit of bondage to put us in fear, and coming to our heart as the Spirit of adoption, to make us cry, "Father, Father"— He cannot go back to His first work again; for, if so, then He must gratify, yea, and also ratify, that profane and popish doctrine of being forgiven today and unforgiven tomorrow, a child of God today and a child of hell tomorrow. But what does the Scripture say? "Now therefore ye are no more strangers and foreigners, but fellow citizens with the saints, and of the household of God, and are built upon the foundation of the apostles and prophets, Jesus Christ Himself being the chief cornerstone; in whom all the building fitly framed together groweth

unto an holy temple in the Lord, and in whom ye
also are built together for an habitation of God
through the Spirit" (Ephesians 2:19–22).

OBJECTION. "But this is contrary to my experience!"

Why, Christian, what is your experience?

"Why, I was at first, as you have said, possessed
with the fear of damnation, and so under the power
of the Spirit of bondage."

Well said, and how was it then?

"Why, after some time of continuance in these
fears, I had the Spirit of adoption sent to me to seal
up to my soul the forgiveness of sins; and so He did.
I was also helped by the same Spirit, as you have said,
to call God 'Father, Father.' "

Well said, and what after that?

"Why, after that I fell into as great fears as ever I
was in before."

ANSWER. All this may be granted, and yet nevertheless what I have said will remain true; for I have
not said that after the Spirit of adoption is come a
Christian shall not again be in as great fears, for he
may have worse than he had at first. But I say that after the Spirit of adoption has come, the Spirit of
bondage, as such, is sent of God no more to put us
into those fears. "For we have not received the Spirit
of bondage again to fear." Let the Word be true,
whatever your experience is. Do you not understand
me?

After the Spirit of God has told me, and also
helped me to believe it, that the Lord, for Christ's
sake, has forgiven my iniquities, He tells me no
more that they are not forgiven. After the Spirit of

God has helped me, through Christ, to call God my Father, He tells me no more that the devil is my father. After He has told me that I am not under the law but under grace, He tells me no more that I am not under grace but under the law, and bound over by it for my sins to the wrath and judgment of God. But this is the fear that the Spirit as the Spirit of bondage works in the soul at first.

QUESTION. Can you give me further reasons to convince me of the truth of what you say?

ANSWER 1. Yes, because, as the Spirit cannot lie, so He cannot overthrow His own order of working, nor yet contradict that testimony that His servants, by His inspiration, have given of His order of working with them.

But He must do the first of these if He says to us (and that after we have received His own testimony that we are under grace) that yet we are under sin, the law, and wrath.

And He must do the second if, after He has gone through the first work on us as a Spirit of bondage to the second as a Spirit of adoption, He would overthrow as a Spirit of bondage again what before He had built as a Spirit of adoption.

And the third must therefore follow. That is, He overthrows the testimony of His servants, for they have said that now we receive the Spirit of bondage again to fear no more—that is, after we, by the Holy Ghost, are enabled to call God "Father, Father."

ANSWER 2. This is evident also because the covenant abides in which the soul is now interested and is everlasting, not upon the supposition of my obedience, but upon the unchangeable purpose of God and the efficacy of the obedience of Christ, whose blood also has confirmed it. It is "ordered in all things, and sure," said David, "for this is all my salvation" (2 Samuel 23:5).

The covenant, then, is everlasting in itself, being established upon so good a foundation, and therefore stands in itself everlastingly bent for the good of those who are involved in it. Hear the tenor of the covenant, and God's attesting of the truth thereof: "This is the covenant that I will make with the house of Israel after those days, saith the Lord. I will put My laws into their mind and write them in their hearts, and I will be to them a God, and they shall be to Me a people; and they shall not teach every man his neighbor, and every man his brother, saying, 'Know the Lord,' for all shall know Me, from the least to the greatest. For I will be merciful to their unrighteousness, and their sins and their iniquities will I remember no more" (Hebrews 8:10–12). Now, if God will do this to those whom He has comprised in His everlasting covenant of grace, then He will remember their sins no more, that is, unto condemnation; for so it is that He forgets them. So the Holy Ghost, who also is one with the Father and the Son, cannot come to us again, even after we are possessed with these glorious fruits of this covenant, as a Spirit of bondage to put us in fear of damnation.

ANSWER 3. The Spirit of God, after it has come to me as a Spirit of adoption, can come to me no more as a Spirit of bondage to put me in fear, that is, with my first fear, because, by that faith that He Himself has wrought in me, to believe and call God

"Father, Father," I am united to Christ, and stand no more in my own sins or performances, but in His glorious righteousness before Him, and before His Father. And He will not cast away a member of His body, of His flesh, and of His bones. Nor will the Spirit of God come as a Spirit of bondage to put me into a grounded fear of damnation who stands complete before God in the righteousness of Christ; for that is an apparent contradiction.

QUESTION. But may He not come again as a Spirit of bondage to put me into my first fears for my good?

ANSWER. The text says the contrary. "For we have not received the Spirit of bondage again to fear." Nor is God so lacking in wisdom that He should say and unsay, do and undo, or else He cannot do good. When we are sons, and have received adoption as children, He does not send the Spirit after that to tell us we are slaves and heirs of damnation, that we are without Christ, without the promise, without grace, and without God in the world; and yet this He must do if the Spirit comes to us after we have received Him as a Spirit of adoption, and puts us, as a Spirit of bondage, in fear as before.

QUESTION. But by what spirit is it, then, that I am brought again into fears, even into the fears of damnation, and so into bondage?

ANSWER. By the spirit of the devil, who always labors to frustrate the faith, hope, and comfort of the godly.

QUESTION. How does that appear?

ANSWER. By the groundlessness of such fears, by the unseasonableness of them, and by the effects of them. Let me look at each of those with you.

• By the groundlessness of such fears. The ground is removed; for a grounded fear of damnation is this: "I am yet in my sins, in a state of nature, under the law, without faith, and so under the wrath of God." This, I say, is the ground of the fear of damnation, the true ground to fear it; but the man of whom we are speaking is one who has the ground of this fear taken away by the testimony and seal of the Spirit of adoption. He is said to be justified, and has, for the truth that this is his condition, received the evidence of the Spirit of adoption and has been thereby enabled to call God "Father, Father." Now he who has received this has the ground of the fear of damnation taken from him. Therefore his fear, I say, being without ground, is false, and so no work of the Spirit of God.

• By the unseasonableness of them. This spirit always comes too late. It comes after the Spirit of adoption has come. Satan is always too soon or too late. If he would have men believe they are children, he would have them believe it while they are slaves, slaves to him and their lusts. If he would have them believe they are slaves, it is when they are sons, and have received the Spirit of adoption, and the testimony, by that, of their sonship before. And this evil is rooted even in his nature: he is a liar, and the father of lies (John 8:44). His lies are not more clearly known to saints than in this: he always labors to contradict the work and order of the Spirit of truth.

• It also appears by the effects of such fears. For there is a great deal of difference between the natural effects of these fears, which are wrought indeed by the Spirit of bondage, and those which are wrought by this spirit of the devil afterwards.

The fears that are wrought by the Spirit of bondage cause us to confess the truth, that we are Christless, graceless, faithless, and so at present (that is, while He is so working) in a sinful and damnable case. But when the spirit of the devil comes, which is after the Spirit of adoption has come, he causes us to lie, that is, to say that we are Christless, graceless, and faithless. Now this, I say, is wholly, and in all the parts of it, a lie, and he is the father of it.

Besides, the direct tendency of the fear that the Spirit of God as a Spirit of bondage works in the soul is to cause us to come repenting home to God by Jesus Christ. But these latter fears tend directly to make a man (he having first denied the work of God, as he will if he falls in with these fears) run quite away from God, and from His grace to Him in Christ, as will evidently appear if you give but a plain and honest answer to these following questions:

QUESTION 1. Do not these fears make you question whether there was ever a work of grace wrought in your soul?

ANSWER. Yes, verily, that they do.

QUESTION 2. Do not these fears make you question whether ever your first fears were wrought by the Holy Spirit of God?

ANSWER. Yes, verily, that they do.

QUESTION 3. Do not these fears make you question whether ever you have had indeed any true comfort from the Word and Spirit of God?

ANSWER. Yes, verily, that they do.

QUESTION 4. Do you not find intermixed with these fears plain assertions that your first comforts were either from your fancy, or from the devil and a fruit of his delusions?

ANSWER. Yes, verily, I do.

QUESTION 5. Do not these fears weaken your heart in prayer?

ANSWER. Yes, that they do.

QUESTION 6. Do not these fears keep you back from laying hold of the promise of salvation by Jesus Christ?

ANSWER. Yes, for I think that if I were deceived before, if I were comforted by a spirit of delusion before, why may it not be so again? So I am afraid to take hold of the promise.

QUESTION 7. Do not these fears tend to harden your heart and make you desperate?

ANSWER. Yes, verily, that they do.

QUESTION 8. Do not these fears hinder you from profiting in hearing or reading the Word?

ANSWER. Yes, verily, for still whatever I hear or read, I think nothing that is good belongs to me.

QUESTION 9. Do not these fears tend to stir up blasphemies in your heart against God?

ANSWER. Yes, to the point of distracting me.

QUESTION 10. Do not these fears make you sometimes think that it is in vain for you to wait upon the Lord any longer?

ANSWER. Yes, verily; and I have many times almost come to the conclusion that I will no longer read, pray, hear, keep company with God's people, or the like.

Well, poor Christian, I am glad that you have so

plainly answered me; but I pray that you look back upon your answer. How much of God do you think is in these things? How much of His Spirit and the grace of His Word? Simply none at all; for these things cannot be the true and natural effects of the workings of the Spirit of God—no, not as a Spirit of bondage. These are not His doings. Do you not see the very paws of the devil in them, yea, in every one of your ten confessions? Is there not palpably high wickedness in every one of the effects of this fear?

I conclude, then, as I began, that the fear that the Spirit of God works as a Spirit of bondage is good and godly not only because of the Author, but also because of the ground and effects. Yet it can last no longer as such, as producing the aforesaid conclusion, than till the Spirit as the Spirit of adoption comes, because then the soul is manifestly taken out of the state and condition into which it had brought itself by nature and sin and is put into Christ, and so by Him into a state of life and blessedness by grace. Therefore, if first fears come again into your soul after the Spirit of adoption has been with you, know they come not from the Spirit of God, but from the spirit of the devil, for they are a lie in themselves, and their effects are sinful and devilish.

OBJECTION. But I also had such wickedness as that in my heart at my first awakening, and therefore, by your argument, neither should that awakening be but from the devil.

ANSWER. So far as such wickedness was in your heart, so far did the devil and your own heart seek to drive you to despair and drown you there. But you have forgotten the question; the question is not whether you were then troubled with such iniquities, but whether your fears of damnation at that time were not just and good because grounded upon your present condition, which was that you were out of Christ, in your sins, and under the curse of the law; and whether now, since the Spirit of adoption has come to you and has you, and has done that for you as has been mentioned, I say, whether you ought for anything whatsoever to give way to the same fear of damnation. It is evident that you ought not because the ground, the cause, is removed.

OBJECTION. But since I was sealed for the day of redemption, I have grievously sinned against God. Have I therefore no cause to fear as before? May not therefore the Spirit of bondage be sent again to put me in fear as at first? Sin was the first cause, and I have sinned now.

ANSWER. No, by no means, "for we have not received the Spirit of bondage again to fear." That is, God has not given it to us, "for God hath not given us the spirit of fear, but of power, and of love, and of a sound mind" (2 Timothy 1:7).

If, therefore, our first fears come upon us again after we have received from God's hands the spirit of love, power, and of a sound mind, they are to be refused, though we have grievously sinned against our God. This is manifest from 1 Samuel 12:20: "Fear not; ye have done all this wickedness." That is, they were not to fear with that fear which would have made them flee from God, as concluding that they were not now His people.

And the reason is that sin cannot dissolve the

covenant which the sons of God, by His grace, have taken. "If his children forsake My law, and walk not in My judgments; if they break My statutes, and keep not My commandments—then will I visit their transgressions with the rod, and their iniquity with stripes. Nevertheless My lovingkindness will I not utterly take from him, nor suffer My faithfulness to fail" (Psalm 89:30–33).

Now if sin does not dissolve the covenant, if sin does not cast me out of this covenant which has been made personally with the Son of God, and into the hands of which, by the grace of God, I am put, then I ought not, though I have sinned, to fear with my first fears.

Again, sin, after the Spirit of adoption has come, cannot dissolve the relation of father and son, of father and child. And this the Church rightly asserted, and that when her heart was under great hardness, when she had the guilt of erring from His ways. "Doubtless Thou art our Father, though Abraham be ignorant of us, and Israel acknowledge us not" (Isaiah 63:16).

That sin does not dissolve the relation of father and son is further evident. "When the fullness of the time was come, God sent forth His Son, made of a woman, made under the law, to redeem them that were under the law, that we might receive the adoption of sons. And because ye are sons, God hath sent forth the Spirit of His Son into your hearts, crying, 'Abba, Father' " (Galatians 4:4–6). Now mark it, you are no more a servant, that is, no more under the law of death and damnation, but a son; and if you are a son, then you are an heir of God through

Christ (Romans 8:17).

Suppose a child grievously transgresses against and offends his father; is the relation between them therefore dissolved? Again, suppose the father scourges and chastens the son for such offenses; is the relation between them therefore dissolved? Yea, suppose the child should now, through ignorance, cry, and say, "This man is now no more my father." Is he therefore now no more his father? Does not everyone see the folly of such arguments? Why, of the same nature is that doctrine that after we have received the Spirit of adoption, the Spirit of bondage is sent to us again to put us in fear of eternal damnation.

Know, then, that your sin, after you have received the Spirit of adoption to cry to God, "Father, Father," is counted as the transgression of a child, not of a slave, and that all that happens to you for that transgression is but the chastisement of a father. "What son is he whom the father chasteneth not?" (Hebrews 12:7).

It is worth observing that the Holy Ghost checks those who, under their chastisements for sin, forget to call God their Father. "Ye have," says Paul, "forgotten the exhortation which speaketh unto you as unto children, 'My son, despise not thou the chastening of the Lord, nor faint when thou art rebuked of Him' " (Hebrews 12:5). Yea, observe yet further that God's chastising of His children for their sin is a sign of grace and love, and not of His wrath and your damnation. Therefore now there is no ground for the aforesaid fear: "For whom the Lord loveth He chasteneth, and scourgeth every son whom He receiveth" (verse 6).

Now, if God would not have those who have received the Spirit of the Son, however He chastises them, to forget the relation that, by the adoption of sons, they stand in to God—and if He checks those who do forget it, when His rod is upon their backs for sin—then it is evident that those fears you have under color of the coming again of the Spirit as a Spirit of bondage, to put you in fear of eternal damnation, are nothing else but Satan disguised, the better to play his pranks upon you.

I will yet give you two or three instances more wherein it will be manifest that, whatever happens to you (I mean as a chastisement for sin after the Spirit of adoption has come), you ought to hold fast by faith the relation of father and son.

The people spoken of by Moses are said to have lightly esteemed the Rock of their salvation (Deuteronomy 32:5), which Rock is Jesus Christ (1 Corinthians 10:4). That is a grievous sin indeed, yet he says, "Is not He thy Father that hath bought thee?" (Deuteronomy 32:6), and then puts them upon considering the days of old.

Those in the prophet Jeremiah's day had played the harlot with many lovers, and done evil things as they could. They had, as another Scripture puts it, gone a-whoring from their God. Yet God calls to them by the prophet saying, "Wilt thou not from this time cry unto Me, 'My Father, Thou art the guide of my youth'? " (Jeremiah 3:4).

Remember also that eminent text before mentioned in 1 Samuel 12:20: "Fear not; ye have done all this wickedness," and labor to maintain faith in your soul of your being a child, it being true that you have received the Spirit of adoption before, and so that you ought not fall under your first fears because the ground of your eternal damnation has been taken away.

Now, from what has been said, let none take courage to live loose lives under a supposition that once in Christ ever in Christ, and that the covenant cannot be broken nor the relation of father and child dissolved; for it is evident that those who do so have not known what it is to receive the Spirit of adoption. It is the spirit of the devil in his own hue who suggests this to them, and who prevails with them to do so. Shall we do evil that good may come? Shall we sin that grace may abound? Or shall we be base in life because God, by grace, has secured us from the wrath to come? God forbid! These conclusions reveal one who is devoid of fear of God indeed, and of the Spirit of adoption too. For what son is he who, because the father cannot break the relation between the father and him, nor suffer sin to do it, will therefore say, "I will live altogether after my own lusts. I will labor to be a continual grief to my father"? What son would do that?

Yet, lest the devil (for some are not ignorant of his devices) should get an advantage against some of the sons, to draw them away from the filial fear of their Father, let me here, to prevent such temptations, present such with these following considerations:

Though God cannot and will not dissolve the relation which the Spirit of adoption has made between the Father and His sons for any sin that such commit, yet He can, and often does, take away from them the comfort of their adoption, not suffering children, while sinning, to have the sweet and comfortable sense thereof on their hearts. He can allow them to be in the state of the unhappy man to whom it is said, "Snares are round about thee, and sudden fear troubleth thee, or darkness, that thou canst not see; and an abundance of waters covers thee" (Job 22:10–11).

God knows how to hide His face from them, and so to afflict them with that dispensation that it shall not be in the power of the world to comfort them. "When He hideth His face, who then can behold Him?" (Job 34:29).

God knows how to make you feel as if you possess again the sins that He long since has pardoned, and that in such a way that things shall be bitter to your soul. "Thou writest bitter things against me," says Job, "and makest me to possess the iniquities of my youth" (Job 13:26). By this also He once made David groan, and pray against it as an insupportable affliction (Psalm 25:7).

God can lay you in the dungeon in chains and roll a stone upon you. He can make your feet fast in the stocks, and make you a laughing stock to men and angels (Lamentations 3:55; Job 13:27).

God knows how to cause to cease the sweet operations and blessed influences of His grace in your soul, and to make those gospel showers that formerly you have enjoyed become now to you nothing but powder and dust (see Deuteronomy 28:24).

God knows how to fight against you with the sword of His mouth, and to make you a butt for His arrows. And this is a most dreadful dispensation (Revelation 2:16; Job 6:4; Psalm 38:2–5).

God knows how to so bow you down with guilt and distress that you shall in no way be able to lift up your head (Psalm 40:12).

God knows how to break your bones, and to make you, by reason of that, live in continual anguish of spirit. Yea, He can send a fire into your bones that shall burn, and none shall be able to quench it (Psalm 51:8; Lamentations 3:4, 1:13; Psalm 102:3; Job 30:30).

God knows how to lay you aside, and make no use of you as to any work for Him in your generation. He can throw you aside as a broken vessel (Psalm 31:12; Ezekiel 44:10–13).

God knows how to kill you, and to take you away from the earth for your sins (1 Corinthians 11:32).

God knows how to plague you in your death with great plagues, and those of long continuance (Psalm 73:14).

What shall I say? God knows how to let Satan loose upon you. When you lay dying, He can license him to assault you with great temptations. He can tell how to make you possess the guilt of all your unkindness towards Him, and that when you, as I said, are going out of the world. He can make it so that your life shall be in continual doubt before you, and not suffer you to take any comfort day or night. Yea, He can drive you even to madness with His chastisements for your folly; and yet all shall be done by Him to you as a father chastises his son (Deuteronomy 28:65–67).

Furthermore, God knows how to tumble you off

your deathbed in a cloud. He can let you die in the dark, so that when you are dying you shall not know where you are going, that is, whether to heaven or to hell. Yea, He knows how to let you seem to come short of life both in your eyes and also in the eyes of those who behold you. "Let us therefore fear," said the apostle, though not with slavish, yet with filial fear, "lest, a promise being left us of entering into His rest, any of you should seem to come short of it" (Hebrews 4:1).

Now, all this, and much more, can God do to His children, as a Father, by His rod and His rebukes. Ah! who knows but those who are under them what terrors, fears, distresses and amazements God can bring His people into? He can put them into a furnace or a fire, and no tongue can tell what else, so unsearchable and fearful are His fatherly chastisements, and yet never give them the Spirit of bondage again to fear. Therefore, if you are a son, take heed of sin, lest all these things overtake you and come upon you.

OBJECTION. But I have sinned, and am under this high and mighty hand of God.

ANSWER. Then you know what I say is true; yet take heed of hearkening unto such temptations as would make you believe you are outside of Christ, under the law, and in a state of damnation. Take heed also that you do not conclude that the author of these fears is the Spirit of God, come to you again as a Spirit of bondage to put you into such fears, lest, unawares to yourself, you deify the devil, dishonor your Father, overthrow good doctrine, and bring yourself into a double temptation.

OBJECTION. But if God deals thus with a man, how can he otherwise think but that he is a reprobate, a graceless, Christless, and faithless man?

ANSWER. Nay, but why do you tempt the Lord your God? Why do you sin and provoke the eyes of His glory? "Wherefore doth a living man complain, a man for the punishment of his sins?" (Lamentations 3:39). He does not willingly afflict nor grieve the children of men; but if you sin, though God should save your soul, as He will if you are an adopted son of God, yet He will make you know that sin is sin. The rod that He will chastise you with, if need be, shall be made of scorpions. Read the whole book of Lamentations; read the complaints of Job and David; yea, read what happened to His Son, His well-beloved, and that when He only stood in the place of sinners, being in Himself altogether innocent. And then consider, O you sinning child of God, if it is any injustice in God, yea, if it is not necessary that you should be chastised for your sin.

But then, I say, when the hand of God is upon you, however grievous it is, take heed and beware that you give not way to your first fears lest, as I said before, you add to your affliction. To help you here, let me give you a few instances of the conduct of some of the saints under some of the most heavy afflictions that they have met with for sin.

Job was in great affliction, and that, as he confessed, for sin. "I have sinned; what shall I do unto Thee, O Thou preserver of men? Why hast Thou set me as a mark against Thee, so that I am a burden to myself?" (Job 7:20). Yet he did not count all this as a

sign of a damnable state, but as a trial and chastisement. And he said, when in the hottest part of this
battle, "When He hath tried me, I shall come forth
as gold" (Job 23:10). And again, when he was pressed
upon by the tempter to think that God would kill
him, he answered with the greatest confidence,
"Though He slay me, yet will I trust in Him" (Job
13:15).

David complained that God had broken his
bones, that He had set His face against his sins, and
had taken from him the joy of his salvation. Yet even
at this time he said, "O God, Thou God of my salvation" (Psalm 51:14).

Heman complained that his soul was full of
troubles, that God had laid him in the lowest pit,
that He had put His acquaintance far from him and
was casting off his soul, had hidden His face from
him, and that he was afflicted from his youth up and
ready to die with trouble. He says, moreover, that the
fierce wrath of God went over him and that His terrors had cut him off, yea, that by reason of them he
was distracted, and yet, even before he makes any of
these complaints, he takes fast hold of God as his,
saying, "O Lord God of my salvation" (Psalm 88).

The Church, in Lamentations, complains that
the Lord had afflicted her for her transgressions,
and that in the day of His fierce anger. They also
said that He had trodden underfoot her mighty
men, and that He had called the heathen against
her. She says that He covered her with a cloud in His
anger, that He was an enemy, and that He had hung
a chain upon her. She adds, moreover, that He had
shut out her prayer, broken her teeth with gravel

stones, and covered her with ashes, and, in conclusion, that He had utterly rejected her. But what does
she do under all this trial? Does she give up her
faith and hope, and return to that fear that begot
the first bondage? No. " 'The Lord is my portion,'
saith my soul; 'therefore will I hope in Him.' " Yea,
she adds, "O Lord, Thou hast pleaded the causes of
my soul; Thou hast redeemed my life" (Lamentations 3:24, 58).

These things show that God's people, even after
they have received the Spirit of adoption, fell foully
into sin, and have been bitterly chastised for it; and
also that when the rod was most smart upon them,
they made great conscience of not giving way to
their first fears wherewith they were made afraid by
the Spirit as it wrought as a Spirit of bondage; for,
indeed, there is no such thing as the coming of the
Spirit of bondage to put us in fear the second time
as such, that is, after He has come as the Spirit of
adoption to the soul.

I conclude, then, that the fear that is wrought by
the Spirit of bondage is good and godly because the
ground for it is sound; and I also conclude that He
comes to the soul as a Spirit of bondage but once,
and that once is before He comes as a Spirit of adoption. And if, therefore, the same fear again takes
hold of your heart—that is, if after you have received
the Spirit of adoption you fear again the damnation
of your soul, that you are outside of Christ and under
the law—that fear is bad and of the devil, and ought
by no means to be admitted by you.

QUESTION. But since it is as you say, how does
the devil, after the Spirit of adoption comes, work

the child of God into those fears of being outside of Christ, not forgiven, and so an heir of damnation again?

ANSWER. 1. By giving the lie, and by prevailing with us to give it too, to the work of grace wrought in our hearts, and to the testimony of the Holy Spirit of adoption.

2. Or by abusing our ignorance of the everlasting love of God toward His people in Christ, and the duration of the covenant of grace.

3. Or by abusing some Scripture that seems to look that way, but does not.

4. Or by abusing our senses and reason.

5. Or by strengthening our unbelief.

6. Or by overshadowing our judgment with horrid darkness.

7. Or by giving us counterfeit representations of God.

8. Or by stirring up and setting in a rage our inward corruptions.

9. Or by pouring into our hearts an abundance of horrid blasphemies.

10. Or by putting wrong constructions on the rod and chastising hand of God.

11. Or by charging upon us that our ill behavior under the rod and chastising hand of God is a sign that we indeed have no grace, but are downright graceless reprobates.

By these things, and others like these, Satan brings the child of God not only to the borders, but even into the bowels of the fears of damnation, after he has received a blessed testimony of eternal life, and that by the Holy Spirit of adoption.

QUESTION. But would you not have the people of God stand in fear of His rod, and be afraid of His judgments?

ANSWER. Yes, and the more they are rightly afraid of them, the less they will come under them; for it is want of fear that brings us into sin, and it is sin that brings into these afflictions. But I would not have them fear with the fear of slaves, for that will add no strength against sin; rather, I would have them fear with the reverential fear of sons, and that is the way to depart from evil.

QUESTION. How is that?

ANSWER. It is, having before received the Spirit of adoption, still to believe that He is our Father, and so to fear with the fear of children and not as slaves fear a tyrant. I would, therefore, have them look upon His rod, rebukes, chidings, and chastisements, and also upon the wrath wherewith He inflicts, to be but the dispensations of their Father.

So believing will maintain, or at least help to maintain, in the heart a son-like bowing under the rod.

It also maintains in the soul a son-like confession of sin, and a justifying of God under all the rebukes He grieves us with. It also engages us to come to Him, to claim and lay hold of former mercies, to expect more, and to hope a good end shall be made of all God's present dispensations towards us.

Now, God would have us thus fear His rod, because He is resolved to chastise us therewith, if so be we sin against Him, as I have already shown; for although God's bowels turn within Him, even while He is threatening His people, yet if we sin He will lay on the rod so hard as to make us cry, "Woe unto us, that we have sinned!" (Lamentations 5:16). And therefore, as I said, we should be afraid of His judgments, yet only as mentioned above, as of the rod, wrath, and judgment of a Father.

QUESTION. But have we any other considerations to move us to fear God with childlike fear?

ANSWER 1. Consider that God thinks it right to have it so, and He is wiser in heart than you. He knows best how to secure His people from sin, and to that end has given them a law and commandments to read that they may learn to fear Him as a Father.

ANSWER 2. Consider that He is mighty in power; if He touches but with a fatherly touch, neither man nor angel can bear it. Yea, Christ makes use of that argument that He has power to cast into hell: "Yea, I say unto you, fear Him" (Luke 12:5).

ANSWER 3. Consider that He is everywhere; you cannot be out of His sight or presence, nor out of the reach of His hand. " 'Fear ye not Me?' saith the Lord" (Jeremiah 5:22). " 'Can any hide himself in secret places that I shall not see him?' saith the Lord. 'Do not I fill heaven and earth?' saith the Lord" (Jeremiah 23:24).

ANSWER 4. Consider that He is holy, and cannot look with liking upon the sins of His own people. Therefore, said Peter, "as obedient children, not fashioning yourselves according to the former lusts in your ignorance, but as He which hath called you is holy, so be ye holy in all manner of conversation; because it is written, 'Be ye holy; for I am holy.' And if ye call on the Father, who without respect of persons judgeth according to every man's work, pass the time of your sojourning here in fear" (1 Peter 1:14–17).

ANSWER 5. Consider that He is good, and has been good to you, good in that He has singled you out from others and saved you from their death and hell, though you perhaps were worse in your life than those He left when He laid hold of you. Oh, how this should engage your heart to fear the Lord all the days of your life! They "shall fear the Lord and His goodness in the latter days" (Hosea 3:5).

And now, for the present, I have done with that fear, I mean as to its first workings, namely to put us in fear of damnation.

Chapter 3

The True Character of the Fear of God

I now come to treat the grace of fear more immediately intended in the text, which I call a lasting godly fear. I shall show how it is described by the Scripture, and what this fear flows from.

First, how this fear is described by the Scripture, and that more generally and more particularly.

More generally. It is called a grace, that is, a sweet and blessed work of the Spirit of grace as He is given to the elect. Hence the apostle says, "Let us have grace, whereby we may serve God acceptably with reverence and godly fear" (Hebrews 12:28); for as the fear that brings bondage is wrought in the soul by the Spirit as a Spirit of bondage, so this fear (which is a fear that we have while we are in the liberty of sons) is wrought by Him as He manifests to us our liberty. "Where the Spirit of the Lord is, there is liberty" (2 Corinthians 3:17), that is, where He is a Spirit of adoption, setting the soul free from that bondage under which it was held by the same Spirit, while He wrought as a Spirit of bondage.

Hence, as He is called a Spirit working bondage to fear, so He, as the Spirit of the Son and of adoption, is called "the Spirit of knowledge and of the fear of the Lord" (Isaiah 11:2). This is because that Spirit of grace is the author, animator, and maintainer of our filial fear, or of that fear that is sonlike, and that subjects the elect unto God, His Word, and His ways as a Father.

This fear is called also "the fear of God," not as that which is ungodly is, nor yet as that may be which is wrought by the Spirit as the Spirit of bondage, but by way of eminence, namely as a dispensation of the grace of the gospel and as a fruit of eternal love. "I will put My fear in their hearts, that they shall not depart from Me" (Jeremiah 32:40).

This fear of God is called "God's treasure," for it is one of His choice jewels; it is one of the rarities of heaven. "The fear of the Lord is His treasure" (Isaiah 33:6). And it may well go under such a title for, like treasure, the fear of the Lord is not found in every corner. It is said that "All men have not faith" (2 Thessalonians 3:2) because that also is more precious than gold. The same is said about this fear: "There is no fear of God before their eyes" (Romans 3:18), that is, the greatest part of men are utterly destitute of this goodly jewel, this treasure, the fear of the Lord. When poor vagrants come straggling to some lord's house, they may perhaps obtain some scraps and fragments; they may also obtain old shoes and some sorry, cast-off rags, but they do not get any of his jewels. They may not touch his choicest treasure, for that is kept for the children and those who shall be his heirs.

We may say the same also of this blessed grace of fear, which is here called God's treasure. It is only bestowed upon the elect, the heirs and children of the promise; all others are destitute of it, and so continue to death and judgment.

This grace of fear is that which makes men exceed and go beyond all men in the account of God.

It is that which beautifies a man and prefers him above all others. "Hast thou," God said to Satan, "considered My servant Job, that there is none like him in the earth, a perfect and an upright man, one that feareth God and escheweth evil?" (Job 1:8).

Mind it, there is none like him, "none like him in the earth." I suppose this passage means either that Job was unique in those parts, or else that he was the man who abounded in the fear of the Lord, and none feared the Lord like him. He exceeded others with respect to his reverencing God, bowing before Him, and sincerely complying with His will; and therefore he is accounted to be the excellent man. It is not the knowledge of the will of God, but our sincerely complying therewith that proves we fear the Lord; and it is our so doing that puts upon us the sign of excellence. Hereby appears our perfection; herein is manifest our uprightness. A perfect and upright man is one who fears God, and manifests it because he avoids evil.

Therefore this grace of fear is that without which no part or piece of service which we do unto God can be accepted by Him. It is, as I may call it, "the salt of the covenant" (Leviticus 2:13), which seasons the heart, and therefore must not be lacking there. It is also that which salts or seasons all our doings, and therefore must not be lacking in any of them.

I take this grace of fear to be that which softens the heart, and which makes it stand in awe of both the mercies and judgments of God. This is that which retains in the heart that due dread and reverence of the heavenly Majesty that it is fitting should both be in and be kept in the heart of poor sinners.

Wherefore, when David described this fear in its exercise, he called it an awe of God. "Stand in awe, and sin not" (Psalm 4:4); and again, "My heart standeth in awe of Thy Word" (Psalm 119:161); and again, "Let all the earth fear the Lord; let all the inhabitants of the world stand in awe of Him" (Psalm 33:8).

This is that, therefore, that is, as I said before, so excellent a thing in the eyes of God, namely a grace of the Spirit, the fear of God, His treasure, the salt of the covenant, that which makes men exceed all others. For it is that which makes the sinner stand in awe of God, which posture is the most comely thing in us throughout all ages.

More particularly. This grace is called the "beginning of knowledge" (Proverbs 1:7) because, by the first gracious discovery of God to the soul, this grace is begotten; and, again, because the first time that the soul apprehends God in Christ to be good unto it this grace is animated, by which the soul is put into a holy awe of God, which causes it with reverence and due attention to hearken to Him and tremble before Him. It is also by virtue of this fear that the soul inquires yet more after the blessed knowledge of God. This is more evident because, where this fear of God is wanting, or where the discovery of God is not attended with it, the heart still abides rebellious, obstinate, and unwilling to know more that it might comply therewith. Nay, for want of it, such sinners say to God, "Depart from us; for we desire not the knowledge of Thy ways" (Job 21:14).

This fear is called "the beginning of wisdom" (Psalm 111:10) because then, and not until then, a man begins to be truly spiritually wise. What wisdom is there where the fear of God is not? Therefore the fools are described thus: "For they hated knowledge, and did not choose the fear of the Lord" (Proverbs 1:29). The Word of God is the fountain of knowledge into which a man will not look with godly reverence until he is endowed with the fear of the Lord. Therefore it is rightly called "the beginning of knowledge; but fools despise wisdom and instruction" (Proverbs 1:7). It is, therefore, this fear of the Lord that makes a man wise for his soul, for life, and for another world. It is this that teaches him how he should escape those spiritual and eternal ruins by which the fool is overtaken and swallowed up forever. As for man devoid of this fear of God, wherever he is wise or in whatever he excels, yet about the matters of his soul there is none more foolish than himself; for through the want of the fear of the Lord he leaves the best things half done, and only pursues with all his heart those that will leave him in the snare when he dies.

This fear of the Lord is to hate evil, to hate sin and vanity. Sin and vanity are the sweet morsels of the fool, and what the carnal appetite of the flesh runs after. And it is only the virtue entailed in fearing the Lord that makes the sinner have an antipathy against it. "By the fear of the Lord men depart from evil" (Proverbs 16:6). That is, men shun, separate themselves from, and avoid it in its appearances. Wherefore it is plain that those who love evil are not possessed with the fear of God.

There is a generation that will pursue evil, that will take it in, nourish it, lay it up in their hearts, hide it, plead for it, and rejoice to do it. These cannot have in them the fear of the Lord, for that is to hate it and to make men depart from it. Where the fear of God and sin are, it will be with the soul as it was with Israel when Omri and Tibni strove to reign among them both at once: one of them must be put to death; they cannot live together. Sin must go down, for the fear of the Lord begs in the soul a hatred against it and an abhorrence of it. Therefore sin must die, that is, as to the affections and lusts of it, for as Solomon says in another case, "Where no wood is, there the fire goeth out" (Proverbs 26:20). So we may say, where there is a hatred of sin, and where men depart from it, there it loses much of its power; it waxes feeble and decays. Therefore Solomon says again, "Fear the Lord, and depart from evil" (Proverbs 3:7). It is as if he had said, "Fear the Lord, and it will follow that you shall depart from evil." Departing from evil is a natural consequence, a proper effect of the fear of the Lord.

By the fear of the Lord men depart from evil, that is, in their judgment, will, mind, and affections. Not that by the fear of the Lord sin is annihilated, or has lost its existence in the soul; there still will be those Canaanites, but they are hated, loathed, abominated, fought against, prayed against, watched against, striven against, and mortified in the soul.

This fear is called a fountain of life. "The fear of the Lord is a fountain of life, to depart from the snares of death" (Proverbs 14:27).

It is a fountain, a spring, which so continually supplies the soul with a variety of considerations of sin, of God, of death, and of life eternal as to keep the soul in continual exercise of virtue and in holy contemplation. It is a fountain of life; every operation thereof, every act and exercise thereof, has a true and natural tendency to spiritual and eternal felicity. Wherefore the wise man says in another place, "The fear of the Lord tendeth to life, and he that hath it shall abide satisfied; he shall not be visited with evil" (Proverbs 19:23). It tends to life even in its nature. Everything has a tendency to that which is most natural to itself: the fire to burn, the water to wet, the stone to fall, the sun to shine, and sin to defile. Thus I say that the fear of the Lord tends to life; the nature of it is to make the soul fear God, close with Christ, and walk humbly before Him.

It is "a fountain of life, to depart from the snares of death." What are the snares of death but sin, the wiles of the devil, from which the fear of God has a natural tendency to deliver you and keep you in the way that tends to life?

This fear of the Lord is called "the instruction of wisdom" (Proverbs 15:33). You heard before that it is the beginning of wisdom, but here you find it called the instruction of wisdom; for indeed it is not only that which makes a man begin to be wise, but to improve, and take advantage of all those helps and means to life which God has afforded to that end, both to his own and to his neighbor's salvation. It is the instruction of wisdom; it will make a man capable of using all his natural parts, all his natural wisdom to God's glory and his own good. There lies, even in many natural things, that which, if we were instructed into it, would yield us a great deal of help in the understanding of spiritual matters; for in wis-

dom God has made all the world. Nor is there anything that God has made, whether in heaven above
or on earth below, but there is couched in it some
spiritual mystery. Men think of this no more than
they do the ground they tread on or the stones that
are under their feet, and all because they do not
have this fear of the Lord. For if they did, it would
teach them to think, even from that knowledge of
God that has by the fear of Him been put into their
hearts, that if He is so great and so good, there must
be an abundance of wisdom in the things He has
made. That fear would also endeavor to find out
what that wisdom is, yes, and give to the soul the instruction of it.

Since it is called the instruction of wisdom, it in-
timates to us that its tendency is to keep all even and
in good order in the soul. When Job perceived that
his friends did not deal with him in an even spirit
and orderly manner, he said that they forsook the
fear of the Almighty (Job 6:14). This fear keeps a
man, even in his words and judgment of things. It
may be compared to the ballast of the ship, and to
the poise of the balance of the scales: it keeps all
even, and also makes us steer our course right with
respect to the things that pertain to God and man.

I come now to the second thing, namely to show
you what this fear of God flows from.

This fear, this grace of fear, this son-like fear of
God, flows from the distinguishing love of God toward His elect. "I will be their God," He says, "and I
will put My fear in their hearts." None obtain it but
those who are enclosed and bound up in that bun-

dle. Therefore, in the same place, they are said to be those who are wrapped up in the eternal or everlasting covenant of God, and so designed to be the people who should be blessed with this fear. "I will make an everlasting covenant with them," says God, "that I will not turn away from them, to do them good; but I will put My fear in their hearts, that they shall not depart from Me" (Jeremiah 32:40). This covenant declares to man that God has, in His heart, distinguishing love for some of the children of men; for He says He will be their God, that He will not leave them, nor yet suffer them to depart finally from Him. Into these men's hearts He puts His fear, this blessed grace, and this rare effectual sign of His love, and of their eternal salvation.

This fear flows from a new heart. This fear is not in men by nature. The fear of devils they may have, as an ungodly fear of God, but this fear is not in any but where there dwells a new heart, which is another fruit and effect of this everlasting covenant, and of this distinguishing love of God. "A new heart also will I give you" (Ezekiel 36:26). A new heart? What is that? Why, the prophet Jeremiah says that it is "a heart to fear Me" (Jeremiah 32:39), a circumcised one, a sanctified one.

So until a man receives a new heart from God, a heart from heaven, he does not have this fear of God in him. Men do not "put new wine into old bottles, else the bottles break and the wine runneth out and the bottles perish; but they put new wine into new bottles, and both are preserved" (Matthew 9:17).

This fear of God must not be, cannot be found in old hearts. Old hearts are not bottles out of which this fear of God proceeds; but it comes from an honest and good heart, from a new one, from such a one that is also an effect of the everlasting covenant, and of the love of God for men.

"I will give them a heart to fear Me." There must in all actions be heart, and without heart no action is good. Nor can there be faith, love, or fear from every kind of heart; they must flow from such a one whose nature is to produce and bring forth such fruit. "For of thorns men do not gather figs, nor of a bramble bush gather they grapes" (Luke 6:44). So from a corrupt heart there cannot proceed such fruit as the fear of God so as to believe in God and love Him.

The heart naturally is "deceitful above all things, and desperately wicked" (Jeremiah 17:9). How then could there flow from such a one the fear of God? It cannot be. He therefore who has not received, at the hands of God, a new heart cannot fear the Lord.

This fear of God flows from a sound impression that the Word of God makes on our souls; for without an impression of the Word there is no fear of God. Hence it is said that God gave to Israel good laws, statutes, and judgments that they might learn them, and, in learning them, learn to fear the Lord their God (Deuteronomy 4:8). Therefore God says, "Gather the people together, men, and women, and children, and the stranger that is within thy gates, that they may hear, and that they may learn, and fear the Lord your God" (Deuteronomy 31:12).

For as man drinks good doctrine into his soul, so he fears God. If he drinks in much, he fears Him greatly; if he drinks in but little, he fears Him but little; if he does not drink it in at all, he does not fear Him at all.

This, therefore, teaches us how to judge who fears the Lord. They are those who learn, and who stand in awe of the Word. Those fear God who have, by the holy Word of God, the very form of that Word engraved upon the face of their souls. But on the contrary, those do not fear God who do not love good doctrine, who give no place in their souls to the wholesome truths of the God of heaven revealed in His testament, but rather despise it and its true professors. For, as I said before, this fear of God flows from a sound impression that the Word of God makes upon the soul; and therefore this godly fear flows from faith. For where the Word makes a sound impression on the soul, by that impression is faith begotten, whence also this fear flows. Therefore, the right hearing of the Word is called "the hearing of faith" (Galatians 3:2). Hence it is said, "By faith Noah, being warned of God of things not seen as yet, moved with fear, prepared an ark to the saving of his house; by which he condemned the world, and became heir of the righteousness which is by faith" (Hebrews 11:7). The word, the warning that he had from God of things not seen as yet, wrought, through faith therein, that fear of God in his heart that made him prepare against unseen dangers, and that he might be an inheritor of unseen happiness.

Therefore, where there is not faith in the Word of God, there can be none of this fear; and where the Word does not make a sound impression on the soul, there can be none of this faith. So that as vices hang together, and are as the links of a chain, dependent one upon another, even so the graces of the Spirit also are the fruits of one another, and have such a dependence on each other that the one cannot be without the other. No faith, no fear of God; devils' faith, devils' fear; saints' faith, saints' fear.

This godly fear also flows from sound repentance for and from sin; godly sorrow works repentance, and godly repentance produces this fear. "For behold, this selfsame thing, that ye sorrowed after a godly sort, what carefulness it wrought in you, yea, what clearing of yourselves, yea, what indignation, yea, what fear" (2 Corinthians 7:11). Repentance is the effect of sorrow, sorrow is the effect of pain, and pain is the effect of faith. Therefore, fear must be an effect of and flow from repentance.

Sinner, do not deceive yourself; if you are a stranger to sound repentance, which stands in sorrow and shame before God for sin, and also in turning from it, you have no fear of God. You have none of this godly fear, for that is the fruit of and flows from sound repentance.

This godly fear also flows from a sense of the love and kindness of God toward the soul. Where there is no sense or hope of the kindness and mercy of God by Jesus Christ, there can be none of this fear, but rather wrath and despair, which produces that fear that is either devilish, or else that which is only wrought in us by the Spirit as a Spirit of bondage. Wherefore the godly fear that I am now treating flows from some sense or hope of mercy from God by Jesus Christ. "If thou, Lord, shouldest mark iniquities, O Lord, who shall stand? But there is forgiveness with Thee, that Thou mayest be feared" (Psalm 130:3–4).

"There is forgiveness with Thee." This the soul has sense of hope in, and therefore fears God. Indeed, nothing can lay a stronger obligation upon the heart to fear God than a sense of or hope in mercy. This begets true tenderness of heart, true godly softness of spirit. This truly endears the affections to God; and in this true tenderness, softness, and endearing of affection for God lies the very essence of this fear of the Lord, as is manifest by the fruit of this fear when we shall come to speak of it.

This fear of God flows from a due consideration of the judgments of God that are to be executed in the world, yea, upon professors of religion too. Yea, further, God's people themselves, I mean, as to themselves, have such a consideration of His judgments towards them as to produce this godly fear.

When God's judgments are in the earth, they effect the fear of His name in the hearts of His own people. "My flesh trembleth for fear of Thee," said David, "and I am afraid of Thy judgments" (Psalm 119:120). When God smote Uzzah, "David was afraid of God that day" (1 Chronicles 13:12). Indeed, many do not regard the works of the Lord, nor take notice of the operation of His hands; and such cannot fear the Lord. But others observe and regard and wisely consider His doings, and the judgments that He executes; and that makes them fear the Lord.

This God Himself suggests as a means to make us fear Him. Hence He commanded the false prophet to be stoned "that all Israel might hear and fear." Hence also He commanded that the rebellious son should be stoned "that all Israel might hear and fear." The false witness was also to have the same judgment of God executed upon him "that all Israel might hear and fear." The man also who did aught presumptuously was to die "that all Israel might hear and fear" (Deuteronomy 13:11; 21:21; 17:13; 19:20).

There is a natural tendency in judgments themselves to beget a fear of God in the heart of any man; but when the observation of the judgments of God is made by him who has a principle of true grace in his soul, that observation being made, I say, by a gracious heart produces a fear of God in the soul of its own nature, namely a gracious or godly fear of God.

This godly fear also flows from a godly remembrance of our former distresses, when we were distressed with our first fears; for though our first fears were begotten in us by the Spirit's working as a Spirit of bondage, and so are not always to be entertained as such, yet even that fear leaves in us, and upon our spirits, that sense and relish of our first awakenings and dread, as also occasions and produces this godly fear. "Take heed to thyself," said God, "and keep thy soul diligently, lest thou forget the things which thine eyes have seen, and lest they depart from thy heart all the days of thy life; but teach them to thy sons, and thy sons' sons" (Deuteronomy 4:9). But what were the things that their eyes had seen that would so condemn them should they be forgotten? The answer is, the things which they saw at Horeb, namely the fire, the smoke, the darkness, the earthquake, and their first awakenings by the law by which they were brought into a

bondage fear—they were to remember this especially. "Especially," said He, "the day that thou
stoodest before the Lord thy God in Horeb, when
the Lord said unto me, 'Gather Me the people together, and I will make them hear My words, that
they may learn to fear Me all the days that they shall
live upon the earth' " (verse 10). The remembrance
of what we saw, felt, feared, and trembled under the
sense of, when our first fears were upon us, is that
which will produce in our hearts this godly, filial
fear.

This godly fear flows from our receiving an answer to prayer, when we supplicated for mercy at the
hand of God. See the proof for this. "If there be in
the land famine, if there be pestilence, blasting,
mildew, locust, or if there be caterpillar; if their enemy besiege them in the land of their cities; whatsoever plague, whatsoever sickness there be; what
prayer and supplication soever be made by any man,
or by all Thy people Israel, which shall know every
man the plague of his own heart, and spread forth
his hands toward this house—then hear Thou in
heaven Thy dwelling-place, and forgive, and do, and
give to every man according to his ways, whose heart
Thou knowest (for Thou, even Thou only, knowest
the hearts of all the children of men); that they may
fear Thee all the days that they live in the land
which Thou gavest unto our fathers" (1 Kings 8:37–
40).

This grace of fear also flows from a blessed conviction of the all-seeing eye of God, that is, from a
belief that He certainly knows the heart, and sees
every one of the turnings and returnings thereof.

This is intimated in the text last mentioned. "Whose heart Thou knowest, that they may fear Thee"; namely so many of them as are or shall be convinced of this. Indeed, without this conviction this godly fear cannot be in us; the want of this conviction made the Pharisees such hypocrites. "Ye are they," said Christ, "which justify yourselves before men; but God knoweth your hearts" (Luke 16:15). The Pharisees were not aware of this; therefore they so much preferred themselves before those who were by far better than themselves. And it is for want of this conviction that men go on in such secret sins as they do, without fear either of God or of His judgments.

This grace of fear also flows from a sense of the impartial judgment of God upon men according to their works. This also is manifest from the text mentioned before: "And give to every man according to his ways," or works, "that they may fear Thee." This is also manifest by 1 Peter 1:17: "And if ye call on the Father, who without respect of persons judgeth according to every man's work, pass the time of your sojourning here in fear." They who have godly conviction of this will fear God, by which fear their hearts are poised and their works directed with trembling, according to the will of God.

Thus you see what a weighty and great grace this grace of the holy fear of God is, and how all the graces of the Holy Ghost yield mutually their help and strength to the nourishment and life of it. You also see how it flows from them all and has a dependence upon every one of them for its due working in the heart of him who has it.

Chapter 4

The Effects of Godly Fear

Having shown you from what godly fear flows, I come now to show you what proceeds or flows from this godly fear of God when it is seated in the heart of man.

1. There flows from this godly fear a devout reverence of God. David says, "God is greatly to be feared in the assembly of the saints" (Psalm 89:7). God, as I have already shown you, is the proper object of godly fear; it is His person and majesty that this fear always causes the eye of the soul to be upon. "Behold," said David, "as the eyes of servants look unto the hand of their masters, and as the eyes of a maiden unto the hand of her mistress, so our eyes wait upon the Lord our God until He has mercy upon us" (Psalm 123:2).

Nothing awes the soul that fears God so much as does the glorious majesty of God. His person is above all things feared by them. "I fear God," said Joseph (Genesis 42:18), that is, "more than any other I stand in awe of Him. He is my dread. He is my fear. I do all my actions as in His presence, as in His sight. I reverence His holy and glorious majesty, doing all things with fear and trembling before Him."

This fear also makes them have a great reverence for His Word; for that also, I told you, was the rule of their fear. "Princes," said David, "have persecuted me without cause; but my heart standeth in awe of Thy

Word" (Psalm 119:161).

From this grace of fear, therefore, flows reverence for the words of God. More than any laws, that man fears the Word; and he fears no law that does not agree therewith.

There flows from this godly fear a tenderness for God's glory. This fear, I say, will cause a man to afflict his soul when he sees that by professors dishonor is brought to the name of God, and to His Word. "Who would not fear Thee, O King of nations?" said Jeremiah, "for to Thee doth it appertain" (Jeremiah 10:7). He speaks it as being affected with that dishonor that by the body of the Jews was continually brought to His name, His Word, and His ways. He also speaks it of a hearty wish that they once would be otherwise minded. The same saying, in effect, John also has in Revelation 15:4: "Who shall not fear Thee, O Lord, and glorify Thy name?" We clearly conclude that godly fear produces a godly tenderness for God's glory in the world, for that pertains to Him; that is, it is due to Him; it is a debt which we owe to Him. "Give unto the Lord," said David, "the glory due unto His name" (Psalm 29:2).

Now, if there is begotten in the heart of the godly by this grace of fear a godly tenderness of the glory of God, then it follows by consequence that where those who have this fear of God see His glory diminished by the wickedness of the children of men, there they are grieved and deeply distressed. "Rivers of waters," said David, "run down mine eyes, because they keep not Thy law" (Psalm 119:136). Let me give you for this these following instances:

How was David provoked when Goliath defied

the God of Israel (1 Samuel 17:45–46)! Also, when
others reproached God, he tells us that such reproach was even as a sword in his bones (Psalm
42:10). David, also, for the love that he had for the
glory of God's Word, ran the hazard and reproach of
all the mighty people (Psalm 89:50). How was
Hezekiah afflicted when Rabshakeh railed upon his
God (Isaiah 37:3–4)! How tender for the glory of God
were Eli, Daniel, and the three children in their day!
Eli died with fear and trembling of heart when he
heard that the ark of God was taken (1 Samuel 4:18).
Daniel ran the danger of the lions' mouths for the
tender love that he had for the Word and worship of
God (Daniel 6:10–16). The three children ran the
hazard of a burning fiery furnace rather than dare to
dishonor the way of their God (Daniel 3:13–30).

This, therefore, is one of the fruits of this godly
fear, namely a reverence of His name and tenderness for His glory.

2. From this godly fear flows a watchfulness. As it
is said of Solomon's servants that they watched
about his bed because of fear in the night (Song of
Solomon 3:8), so it may be said of those who have
this godly fear that it makes them a watchful people.

It makes them watch their hearts and take heed
to keep them with all diligence, lest they should, by
one or another of the evil one's sleights, be led to
do that which in itself is wicked.

It makes them watch lest some temptation from
hell should enter into their heart to destroy them.

It makes them watch their mouths and keep
them also, sometimes as with a bit and bridle, so
that they offend not with their tongue, knowing that

the tongue is apt, being an evil member, soon to catch the fire of hell to defile the whole body (James 3:2–10).

It makes them watch over their ways, look well to their goings, and make straight paths for their feet (Psalm 39:1; Hebrews 12:13).

Thus this godly fear puts the soul upon its watch lest, from the heart within, from the devil without, from the world or some other temptation, something should surprise and overtake the child of God to defile him or cause him to defile the ways of God, and so offend the saints, open the mouths of men, and cause the enemy to speak reproachfully of religion.

3. There flows from this fear a holy provocation to a reverential fellowship with saints in their religious and godly assemblies, for their further progress in the faith and way of holiness. Malachi 3:16: "Then they that feared the Lord spake often one to another." They spoke of God, His holy and glorious name, His kingdom and works, for their mutual edification. "And a book of remembrance was written before Him for them that feared the Lord, and that thought upon His name."

The fear of the Lord in the heart provokes to this in all its acts, not only of necessity but of nature. It is the natural effect of this godly fear to exercise the Church in the contemplation of God, together and apart. All fear, good and bad, has a natural propensity in it to incline the heart to contemplate the object of fear, and though a man should labor to remove his thoughts from the object of his fear, whether that object were men, hell, devils, or whatever, yet, do what he can, the next time his fear was aroused, it would return again to its object. And so it is with godly fear: it will make a man speak of and think upon the name of God reverentially. Yea, it will make him exercise himself in the holy thoughts of God in such a way that his soul shall be sanctified and seasoned with such meditations.

Indeed, holy thoughts of God, such as you see this fear exercises the heart with, prepare the heart to and for God. This fear, therefore, is what David prayed for on behalf of the people when he said, "O Lord God of Abraham, Isaac, and of Israel, our fathers, keep this forever in the imagination of the thoughts of the heart of Thy people, and prepare their heart unto Thee" (1 Chronicles 29:18).

4. There flows from this fear of God great reverence for His majesty, in and under the use and enjoyment of God's holy ordinances. His ordinances are His courts and palaces, His walks and places where He gives His presence to those who wait upon Him in them, in the fear of His name. And this is the apostle's meaning: "Then had the churches rest throughout all Judea and Galilee and Samaria, and were edified; and walking in the fear of the Lord, and in the comfort of the Holy Ghost, they were multiplied" (Acts 9:31).

The word translated "and walking" intends their use of the ordinances of God. "Walking in all the commandments and ordinances of the Lord blameless" (Luke 1:6). In Old Testament language, this is called "treading God's courts" and "walking in His paths." This, says the text, they did here "in the fear of the Lord," that is, in a great reverence for that

God whose ordinances they were. "Ye shall keep My sabbaths and reverence My sanctuary. I am the Lord" (Leviticus 19:30).

It is one thing to be conversant in God's ordinances, and another to be conversant in them with a due reverence for the majesty and name of that God whose ordinances they are. It is common for men to do the first, but none can do the last without this fear. "In thy fear," said David, "will I worship" (Psalm 5:7). It is this fear of God, therefore, from whence flows that great reverence that His saints have in them for His majesty in and under the use and enjoyment of God's holy ordinances. Consequently, that makes our service in the performance of them acceptable to God through Christ.

For God expects that we serve Him with fear and trembling, and it is odious among men for a man, in the presence or about the service of his prince, to behave himself lightly and without due reverence of that majesty in whose presence and about whose business he is. And if so, how can their service to God have anything like acceptance from the hand of God that is done not in, but without the fear of God! This service must be an abomination to Him, and these servers must come off with rebuke.

5. There flows from this godly fear of God self-denial, that is, a holy abstaining from those things that are either unlawful or inexpedient. Nehemiah 5:15: "The former governors that had been before me were chargeable unto the people, and had taken of them bread and wine, beside forty shekels of silver; yea, even their servants bore rule over the people; but so did not I because of the fear of God."

Here now was self-denial: he would not do as they did who went before him, neither himself, nor should his servants; but what was it that put him upon these acts of self-denial? The answer is the fear of God: "But so did not I because of the fear of God."

Now whether by the fear of God in this place is meant His Word or the grace of fear in his heart may perhaps be a scruple to some, but in my judgment the text must have respect to the latter, namely to the grace of fear; for without that indeed in the heart, the Word will not produce that good self-denial in us of which here you find this good man lived in the daily exercise.

The fear of God, therefore, was the cause of his self-denial; it was this grace of fear in his heart. This made him, as was said before, tender for the honor of God and the salvation of his brother. Yea, he was so tender that rather than give occasion to the weak to stumble or be offended, he would even deny himself that which others never hesitated to do. Paul, also, through the sanctifying operations of this fear of God in his heart, denied himself even lawful things for the profit of his brother. "I will eat no flesh while the world standeth, lest I make my brother to offend" (1 Corinthians 8:13), that is, if his eating it would offend his brother.

Men who do not have this fear of God in them will not, cannot deny themselves (out of love for God, and the good of the weak, who are subject to stumbling at indifferent things); but where this grace of fear is, self-denial follows. There men are tender of offending, and consider that it far better becomes their profession to be of a self-denying, condescending conversation and temper than to insist sturdily on their own liberty in things inexpedient, no matter who is offended thereby.

This grace of fear, therefore, is a very excellent thing because it yields such excellent fruit as this. For as for this self-denial, of however little esteem it is with some, yet the want of it, if the words of Christ are true, as they are, takes quite away from even a professor the very name of a disciple (Matthew 10:37–38; Luke 14:27).

Nehemiah 5:15 says that "they lorded it over the brethren, but so did not I. They took bread and wine, and forty shekels of silver from them, but so did not I; yea, even their servants bore rule over the people, but so did not I, because of the fear of God."

6. There flows from this godly fear of God "singleness of heart" (Colossians 3:22), singleness of heart both to God and man. Singleness of heart is that which, in another place, is called "sincerity" and "godly simplicity." It is when a man does something simply for the sake of Him, or because the law commands it, without respect to some secondary motive, or desire for praise or glory from others. I say, it is when our obedience to God is done simply or only for God's sake, for His Word's sake, without any regard to this or that purpose or personal benefit, "not with eye-service, as men-pleasers, but with singleness of heart, fearing God." A man is more subject to nothing than to swerve from singleness of heart in his service to God and obedience to His will.

How does the Lord charge the children of Israel, and all their obedience, and that for seventy years

together, with the want of singleness of heart towards Him! "When ye fasted and mourned in the
fifth and seventh month, even those seventy years,
did ye at all fast unto Me, even to Me? And when ye
did eat, and when ye did drink, did not ye eat for
yourselves, and drink for yourselves?" (Zechariah
7:5–6).

They lacked this singleness of heart in their fast-
ing and eating, in their mourning and drinking;
they had double hearts in what they did. They did
not do as the apostle bade, "Whether therefore ye
eat, or drink, or whatsoever ye do, do all to the glory
of God" (1 Corinthians 10:31). And the reason for
their failure was that they lacked this fear of God; for
that, as the apostle here says, effects singleness of
heart toward God, and makes a man, as John said of
Gaius, do faithfully whatever he does (3 John 5). And
the reason is, as has been already urged, that that
grace of fear of God retains and keeps upon the
heart a reverential and awful sense of the dreadful
majesty and all-seeing eye of God. It also keeps a due
consideration of the day of account before him; it
likewise makes his service sweet and pleasing, and
fortifies the soul against all discouragements. By
this means, I say, the soul, in its service to God or
man, is not so soon captivated as where there is not
this fear; but through it and by it its service is accepted, being single, sincere, simple, and faithful,
while others, with what they do, are cast into hell for
their hypocrisy, for they mix not what they do with
godly fear.

Singleness of heart in the service of God is of
such absolute necessity that without it, as I have

hinted, nothing can be accepted, because where that is wanting there wants love for God, and for that which is true holiness indeed. It was this singleness of heart that made Nathanael so honorable in the eyes of Jesus Christ. "Behold," said He, "an Israelite indeed, in whom is no guile" (John 1:47). And it was the want of it that made Him so much abhor the Pharisees. They wanted sincerity, simplicity, and godly sincerity in their souls, and so became an abhorrence in His esteem. Now, I say this golden grace, this singleness of heart, flows from this godly fear of God.

7. There flows from this godly fear of God compassion and caring for those saints who are in need and distress. This is manifest in Obadiah. It is said of him that he "took an hundred prophets, and hid them by fifty in a cave, and fed them with bread and water" (1 Kings 18:4); and this was in the days when Jezebel, that tyrant, sought to destroy them. But what was it that so moved his heart as to cause him to do this thing? Why, it was this blessed grace of the fear of God. "Now Obadiah," says the text, "feared the Lord greatly; for it was so, when Jezebel cut off the prophets of the Lord, that Obadiah took an hundred prophets, and hid them by fifty in a cave, and fed them with bread and water." This was charity to the distressed, even to the distressed for the Lord's sake.

Had Obadiah not feared the Lord, yea, had he not greatly feared Him, he would not have been able to do this thing, especially as the case then stood with him, and also with the Church at that time; for then Jezebel sought to slay all who indeed feared the

Lord. Yea, and the persecution prevailed so much at that time that even Elijah himself thought that she had killed all but him. But now the fear of God in this good man's heart put itself forth into acts of mercy, though attended with so imminent danger.

See here, therefore, that the fear of God will put forth itself in the heart where God has put it to show kindness and have compassion upon the distressed servants of God, even in the very neighborhood of Jezebel's court; for Obadiah dwelt in Ahab's house, and Jezebel was Ahab's wife, and a horrible persecutor, as was said before. Yet Obadiah would show mercy to the poor because he feared God; yea, he would venture her displeasure, his place, and neck, and all, but he would be merciful to his brethren in distress.

Cornelius, also, being a man possessed with this fear of God, became a very free-hearted and open-handed man to the poor. He feared God and gave much alms to the people. Indeed, this fear, this godly fear of God, is a universal grace; it will stir up the soul unto all good duties. It is a fruitful grace; from it ever flows an abundance of excellent virtues, nor without it can anything be done well that is done.

8. There flows from this fear of God hearty, fervent, and constant prayer. This also is seen in Cornelius, that devout man. He "feared God." And what then? Why, he "gave much alms to the people, and prayed to God always" (Acts 10:2).

Did I say that hearty, fervent, and constant prayer flowed from this fear of God? I will add that if the whole duty, and the continuation of it, is not managed with this fear of God, it profits nothing at all. It is said of our Lord Jesus Christ Himself, "He was heard in that He feared" (Hebrews 5:7). He prayed, then, because He feared, because He feared God, and therefore His prayer was accepted because He feared.

This godly fear is so essential to right prayer, and right prayer is such an inseparable effect and fruit of this fear, that you must have both or none. He who prays not fears not God; yet he who prays not fervently and frequently fears Him not; and so he who fears Him not cannot pray. For if prayer is the effect of this fear of God, then without this fear prayer, fervent prayer, ceases. How can those pray or make conscience of the duty who fear not God? O prayerless man, you fear not God! You would not live so long like a swine or a dog in the world as you do if you feared the Lord.

9. There flows from this fear of God a readiness and willingness, at God's call, to give up our best enjoyments to His disposal. This is evident in Abraham who, at God's call, without delay, rose early in the morning to offer up his only and well-beloved Isaac as a burnt offering in the place God appointed.

It was a rare thing that Abraham did; and had he not had this rare grace, this fear of God, he would not, he could not, have done to God's liking so wonderful a thing. It is true that the Holy Ghost also makes this service of Abraham's to be the fruit of his faith. "By faith Abraham, when he was tried, offered up Isaac; and he that had received the promises offered up his only begotten son" (Hebrews 11:17). Aye, and without doubt, love for God in Abraham was not wanting in his service, nor was this grace of fear. Nay, in the history where it is recorded it is chiefly accounted as the fruit of his godly fear, and that by an angel from heaven. "And the angel of the Lord called unto him out of heaven and said, 'Abraham, Abraham'; and he said, 'Here am I.' And he said, 'Lay not thine hand upon the lad, neither do thou anything unto him; for now I know that thou fearest God, seeing thou hast not withheld thy son, thine only son from Me' " (Genesis 22:11–12).

It is as if God had said, "Now I know it; now you have offered up your only Isaac, your all, at the bidding of your God. Now I know it." The fear of God is not presently discerned in the heart and life of a man. Abraham had long before this done many a holy duty, and showed much willingness of heart to observe and do the will of God; yet you find not, as I remember, that he had this testimony from heaven that he feared God till now. But now he has it; now he has it from heaven. "Now I know that thou fearest God." Many duties may be done (though I do not say that Abraham did them) without the fear of God; but when a man shall not protest or withhold his darling from God, when called upon by God to offer it up to Him, that declares, yea, and gives conviction to angels that now he fears God.

10. There flows from this godly fear humility of mind. This is evident because, when the apostle cautions the Romans against the venom of spiritual pride, he directs them to the exercise of this blessed grace of fear as its antidote. "Be not high-minded," he says, "but fear" (Romans 11:20). Pride, spiritual pride, which is here set forth by the word "high-

minded," is a sin of a very high and damnable nature. It was the sin of the fallen angels, and is that
which causes men to fall into the same condemnation. "Lest being lifted up with pride he fall into the
condemnation of the devil" (1 Timothy 3:6). Pride, I
say, condemns a professor with the damnation of
devils, with the damnation of hell, and therefore it
is a deadly, deadly sin. Now, against this deadly sin is
set the grace of humility, that comely garment, for
so the apostle calls it, saying, "Be clothed with humility" (1 Peter 5:5).

But the question is now, how do we attain to and
live in the exercise of this blessed and comely grace?
To this the apostle answers, "Fear. Be afraid with
godly fear; and from there will flow humility. Be not
highminded, but fear."

That is, fear, or be continually afraid and jealous
of yourselves, and of your own naughty hearts; also
fear lest, at some time or other, the devil, your adver-
sary, should get advantage over you. Fear, lest, by
forgetting what you are by nature, you also forget the
need that you have of continual pardon, support,
and supplies from the Spirit of grace, and so grow
proud of your own abilities, or of what you have received from God, and fall into condemnation of the
devil. Fear, and that will make you little in your own
eyes, keep you humble, put you upon crying to God
for protection, and upon lying at His footstool for
mercy; that will also make you have low thoughts of
your own parts, your own doings, and cause you to
prefer your brother before yourself. And so you will
walk in humiliation and be continually under the
teachings of God, and under His conduct in your

way. God will teach the humble. "The meek will He guide in judgment, and the meek will He teach His way" (Psalm 25:9).

From this grace of fear, then, flows this excellent and comely thing known as humility; yea, it also is maintained by this fear. Fear keeps a man from trusting in himself; it puts a man upon trying all things; it puts a man upon desiring counsel and help from heaven; it makes a man ready and willing to hear instruction, and makes a man walk lowly, softly, and so securely in the way.

11. There flows from this grace of fear hope in the mercy of God. "The Lord taketh pleasure in them that fear Him, in those that hope in His mercy" (Psalm 147:11). The latter part of the text is an explanation of the former, as if the psalmist had said, "These are the men who fear the Lord, even those who hope in His mercy." For true fear produces hope in God's mercy.

And it is further manifested thus: fear, true fear of God, inclines the heart to a serious inquiry after that way of salvation which God Himself has prescribed. Now the way that God has appointed by which the sinner is to obtain the salvation of his soul is His mercy as set forth in the Word; and godly fear has special regard to the Word. To this way, therefore, the sinner with this godly fear submits his soul, rests himself upon it, and so is delivered from the death into which others, for want of this fear of God, fall headlong.

It is, as I also hinted before, the nature of godly fear to be greatly setting the soul to inquire which is and which is not the thing approved of God, and ac-

cordingly to embrace it or shun it. Now, I say, this
fear, having put the soul upon a strict and serious
inquiry after the way of salvation, at last finds it to be
by the mercy of God in Christ. Therefore this fear
puts the soul upon hoping also in Him for eternal
life and blessedness, by which hope he not only secures his soul, but becomes a person in whom God
delights. "The Lord taketh pleasure in them that
fear Him, in those that hope in His mercy" (Psalm
147:11).

Besides, this godly fear carries in it self-evidence
that the state of the sinner is happy because he is
possessed with this happy grace. Therefore, as John
says, "We know that we have passed from death unto
life, because we love the brethren" (1 John 3:14). So
it is here: "The Lord taketh pleasure in them that
fear Him, in those that hope in His mercy." If I fear
God, and if my fearing of Him is a thing in which
He takes such pleasure, then I may boldly venture to
entrust myself for eternal life into the bosom of His
mercy, which is Christ.

This fear also produces hope. If, therefore, poor
sinner, you know yourself to be one who is possessed
with this fear of God, allow yourself to be persuaded
therefore to hope in the mercy of God for salvation;
for the Lord takes pleasure in you, and it delights
Him to see you hope in His mercy.

12. There flows from this godly fear of God an
honest and conscientious use of all those means
which God has ordained that we should be conversant in for attaining salvation. Faith and hope in
God's mercy secures our justification and hope, and,
as you have heard, they flow from this fear. But now,

besides faith and hope, there is a course of life in those things in which God has ordained us to have our conversation, without which there is no eternal life. "Ye have your fruit unto holiness, and the end everlasting life" (Romans 6:22). "Holiness, without which no man shall see the Lord" (Hebrews 12:14). Not that faith and hope are deficient, if they are right, but they are both counterfeit when not attended with a reverent use of all the means. The soul is put upon the reverent use of them by this grace of fear. "Wherefore, my beloved," said Paul, "as ye have always obeyed, not as in my presence only, but now much more in my absence, work out your salvation with fear and trembling" (Philippians 2:12).

There is a faith and hope of mercy that may deceive a man because they are alone, and not attended with those companions that accompany salvation. But now this godly fear carries in itself not only a moving of the soul to faith and hope in God's mercy, but an earnest provocation to the holy and reverent use of all the means that God has ordained for a man to depend on in order to achieve his eternal salvation.

"Work out your salvation with fear." Not that work is meritorious, or such that it can purchase eternal life; for eternal life is obtained by hope in God's mercy. But this hope, if it is right, is attended with this godly fear, which puts the soul upon a diligent use of all those means that may tend to the strengthening of hope, and so to make us holy in all manner of conversation so that we may be "meet to be partakers of the inheritance of the saints in light." For hope purifies the heart, if fear of God is its companion, and so makes a man a vessel of mercy prepared unto glory. Paul bids Timothy to flee pride, covetousness, doting about questions and the like, and to "follow after righteousness, godliness, faith, love, patience, meekness. Fight the good fight of faith, lay hold of eternal life" (1 Timothy 6:11–12).

So Peter says, "Add to your faith virtue; and to virtue knowledge; and to knowledge temperance; and to temperance patience; and to patience godliness; and to godliness brotherly kindness; and to brotherly kindness charity. For if these things be in you, and abound, they make you that ye shall neither be barren nor unfruitful in the knowledge of our Lord Jesus Christ. Wherefore the rather, brethren, give diligence to make your calling and election sure; for if ye do these things, ye shall never fail; for so an entrance shall be ministered unto you abundantly into the everlasting kingdom of our Lord and Savior Jesus Christ" (2 Peter 1:5–11). The sum of all this is that which was mentioned before, namely to work out our own salvation with fear and trembling. For none of these things can be conscientiously done but by and with the help of this blessed grace of fear.

13. There flows from this godly fear a great delight in the holy commands of God; that is, a delight to be conformable to them. "Blessed is the man that feareth the Lord, that delighteth greatly in His commandments" (Psalm 112:1). This confirms that which was said before, namely that this fear provokes to a holy and reverent use of the means; for that cannot be when there is not a holy, yea, a great delight in the commandments. Wherefore this fear

makes the sinner abhor that which is sin because it is contrary to the object of his delight. A man cannot delight himself at the same time in things directly opposite one to another, such as sin and the holy commandments are. Therefore Christ says of the servant that he "cannot love God and mammon." If he cleaves to one, he must hate and despise the other. There cannot, at the same time, be service to both because they are at enmity one with the other; and so are sin and the commandment. Therefore, if a man delights himself in the commandment, he hates that which is opposite, which is sin; how much more when he greatly delights in the commandment!

Now, this holy fear of God takes the heart and affections from sin, and sets them upon the holy commandment; therefore such a man is rightly esteemed blessed. For no profession makes a man blessed but that which is accompanied with an alienation of the heart from sin. Nor does anything do that when this holy fear is wanting. It is from this fear, then, that love for and delight in the holy commandment flow; and so by that the sinner is kept from those falls and dangers of miscarrying that other professors are so subject to. He greatly delights in the commandment.

14. There flows from this fear of God enlargement of heart. "Then thou shall see, and flow together, and thine heart shall fear, and be enlarged" (Isaiah 60:5). "Thine heart shall fear, and be enlarged": enlarged Godward, enlarged to His ways, enlarged to His holy people, enlarged in love after the salvation of others. Indeed, when this fear of

God is wanting, though the profession be ever so famous, the heart is shut up and straitened, and nothing is done in that princely free spirit which is called "the spirit of the fear of the Lord" (Isaiah 11:2). But with grudging, legally or with desire of vain glory, this enlargedness of heart is wanting, for that flows from this fear of the Lord.

Thus have I shown you what this fear of God is, what it flows from, and also what flows from it.

Chapter 5

The Privileges of Those Who Fear the Lord

Having thus briefly handled, in particular, this fear of God, I shall now show you certain excellent privileges those have who fear the Lord. Not that they are not privileges that have been already mentioned; for what greater privilege is there than to have this fear producing in the soul such excellent things so necessary for us for good, both with reference to this world and that which is to come. But because those fourteen effects set forth in the preceding chapter rather flow from this grace of fear, where it is present, than from a promise to the person who has it, therefore I have chosen rather to discourse of them as the fruits and effects of fear than otherwise. Now, besides all these, there are entailed by promise to the man who has this fear many other blessed privileges, which I shall now, in a brief way, lay open to you.

1. First, that man who fears the Lord has a grant and a license to trust in the Lord with an affirmation that the Lord is his help and his shield. "Ye that fear the Lord, trust in the Lord: He is their help and their shield" (Psalm 115:11). Now, what a privilege is this! An exhortation in general to sinners as sinners, to trust in Him, is a privilege great and glorious; but for a man to be singled out from his neighbors, for a man to be spoken to from heaven, as it were, by name, and to be told that God has

given him a license, a special and peculiar grant to trust in Him, is abundantly more; and yet this is the grant that God has given that man. He has, I say, a license to do it, a license dictated by the Holy Ghost, and left upon record for those to be born who shall fear the Lord to trust in Him. And not only so, but, as the text affirms, He is their help and their shield, their help under all their weaknesses and infirmities and their shield to defend them against all the assaults of the devil and this world. So then, the man who fears the Lord is licensed to make the Lord his stay, and the God of his salvation the succor and deliverer of his soul. He will defend him because His fear is in his heart. Oh, you servants of the Lord, you who fear Him, live in the comfort of this; boldly make use of it when you are in straits, and put your trust under the shadow of His wings, for indeed He would have you do so because you fear the Lord.

2. God has also proclaimed, concerning the man who fears the Lord, that He will also be his teacher and guide in the way that he shall choose; and He has moreover promised concerning such that their soul shall dwell at ease. "What man is he that feareth the Lord?" said David; "him shall He teach in the way that he shall choose" (Psalm 25:12).

Now to be taught of God, what is like it? Yea, what is like being taught in the way that you shall choose? You have chosen the way to life, God's way, but perhaps your ignorance about it is so great, and those who tempt you to turn aside so many and so subtle that they seem to outwit you and confound you with their guile. Well, but the Lord whom you fear will not leave you to your ignorance, nor yet to your enemies' power or subtlety, but will take it upon Himself to be your teacher and your guide in the way that you have chosen. Hear, then, and behold your privilege, O you who fear the Lord; and whoever wanders, turns aside, or swerves from the way of salvation, whoever is lost in the midst of darkness, you shall find the way to the heaven and the glory that you have chosen.

Further, He not only says that He will teach those the way (for that must of necessity be supplied), but He says also that He will teach such *in* it. "Him shall He teach in the way that he shall choose." This argues that as you shall know the way, so the way shall be made, by the communion that you shall have with God therein, sweet and pleasant to you. For this text promises to the man who fears the Lord the presence, company, and discovery of the mind of God while he is going in the way that he has chosen. It is said that the good scribe is instructed *unto* as well as *into* the way of the kingdom of God (Matthew 13:52). That is, he has the heart and mind of God still revealed to him in the way that he has chosen, even all the way from this world to that which is to come, until he shall come to the very gate and door of heaven. What the disciples said was the effect of the presence of Christ, namely that their hearts burned within them while He talked to them by the way (Luke 24:32), shall be also fulfilled in you. He will meet with you in the way, talk with you in the way. He will teach you in the way that you shall choose.

3. Do you fear the Lord? He will open His secret to you, even that which He has hidden and kept se-

cret from all the world, namely the secret of His covenant and your concern therein. "The secret of the Lord is with them that fear Him; and He will show them His covenant" (Psalm 25:14). This, then, further confirms what was said before: His secret shall be with them, and His covenant shall be shown to them.

His secret is that which has been kept hidden from ages and generations, that which He manifests only to the saints or holy ones; that is, His Christ, for He it is who is hidden in God, and whom no man can know but he to whom the Father shall reveal Him.

But, oh! what is wrapped up in this Christ, this secret of God? Why, all the treasures of life, heaven, and happiness. "In whom are hid all the treasures of wisdom and knowledge" (Colossians 2:3), yea, "in Him dwelleth all the fullness of the Godhead bodily" (verse 9).

He also is that hidden One who is so full of grace to save sinners, and so full of truth and faithfulness to keep promise and covenant with them, that their eyes must convey, even by every glance they make upon His person, offices, and relation, such affecting ravishments to the heart that it would please those who see Him to be killed with that sight.

This secret of the Lord shall be, nay, is with those who fear Him, for He dwells in their heart by faith. "And He will show them His covenant," that is, the covenant that is confirmed by God in Christ, that everlasting and eternal covenant. And He will show him too that he is wrapped up therein as in a bundle of life with the Lord his God. These are the thoughts, purposes, and promises of God to those who fear Him.

4. Do you fear the Lord? His eye is always over you for good, to keep you from all evil. "Behold, the eye of the Lord is upon them that fear Him, upon them that hope in His mercy, to deliver their soul from death, and to keep them alive in famine" (Psalm 33:18–19).

His eye is upon them, that is, to watch over them for good. "He that keepeth Israel shall neither slumber nor sleep" (Psalm 121:4). His eyes are upon them, and He will keep them as a shepherd does his sheep from those wolves that seek to devour them and to swallow them up in death. His eyes are upon them, for they are the objects of His delight, the rarities of the world in whom is all His delight. His eye is upon them, as I said before, to teach and instruct them. "I will instruct thee and teach thee in the way which thou shalt go. I will guide thee with Mine eye" (Psalm 32:8). The eye of the Lord, therefore, is upon them—not to take advantage of them, to destroy them for their sins, but to guide, to help and deliver them from death, from that death that would feed upon their souls. "To deliver their soul from death, and to keep them alive in famine" (Psalm 33:19).

Take death here for spiritual and eternal death, and the famine here not for that which comes for want of bread and water, but for that which comes on many for want of the Word of the Lord. The sense is this: The man who fears the Lord shall neither die spiritually nor eternally, for God will keep him with His eye from all those things that would in such a manner kill him. Again, should there be a famine of the Word, should there be a lack both of the Word and those who preach it in the place where you dwell, yet bread shall be given you, and your water shall be sure; you shall not die of famine because you fear God. I say that man shall not, behold, he shall not, because he fears God; and this the next point yet more fully manifests.

5. Do you fear God? Fear Him for this advantage more and more. "O fear the Lord, ye His saints; for there is no want to them that fear Him. The young lions do lack, and suffer hunger; but they that seek the Lord shall not want any good thing" (Psalm 34:9–10). Nothing that God sees good for them shall those men want who fear the Lord. If health will do them good, if sickness will do them good, if riches will do them good, if poverty will do them good, if life will do them good; if death will do them good, then they shall not want them. Neither shall any of these come near them if they will not do them good.

"The lions," that is, the wicked people of the world who do not fear God, are not made sharers in this great privilege; all things fall out to them contrary, because they do not fear God. In the midst of their sufficiency they are in want of that good that God puts into the worst things that the man who fears God meets with in the world.

6. Do you fear God? He has given charge to the armies of heaven to look after, take charge of, to encamp about and deliver you. "The angel of the Lord encampeth round about them that fear Him, and delivereth them" (Psalm 34:7). This also is a privilege entailed to those who in all generations fear the Lord. The angels, the heavenly creatures, have a

commission to take charge of those who fear the Lord; and one of them was able to slay in one night 185,000 men. These are they who encamped about Elisha like horses of fire and chariots of fire when the enemy came to destroy him. They also helped Hezekiah against the band of the enemy because he feared God (2 Kings 6:17; Isaiah 37:36).

The angel of the Lord encamps round about them lest the enemy should set upon them on any side; but let him come where he will, behind or before, on this side or that, the angel of the Lord is there to defend them.

"The angel" is spoken in the singular number, perhaps to show that everyone who fears God has His angel to attend to him and serve him. When the church in the book of Acts was told that Peter stood at the door and knocked, at first they counted the messenger mad; but when she constantly affirmed it, they said, "It is his angel" (Acts 12:15). So Christ says of the children who came to Him, "Their angels do always behold the face of My Father which is in heaven" (Matthew 18:10). "Their angels"—that is, those of them who feared God each had his angel who had a charge from God to keep them safe. We little think of this, yet this is the privilege of those who fear the Lord; yea, if need be they shall all come down to help them and to deliver them rather than that, contrary to the mind of their God, they should by any be abused. "Are they not all ministering spirits, sent forth to minister for them who shall be heirs of salvation?" (Hebrews 1:14).

QUESTION. But how do they deliver them? For the text says, "The angel of the Lord encampeth about them that fear Him, and delivereth them."

ANSWER. The way that they take to deliver those who fear the Lord is sometimes by smiting their enemies with blindness so that they may not find them. And so they served the enemies of Lot (Genesis 19:11). Sometimes they deliver them by smiting them with deadly fear, as they served those who laid siege against Samaria (2 Kings 7:6), and sometimes by smiting their enemies with death itself. Thus they served Herod after he had attempted to kill the Apostle James, and also sought to vex certain others of the church (Acts 12:23). These angels who are servants to those who fear the Lord are those who will, if God asks them, avenge the quarrel of His servants upon the stoutest monarch on earth.

This, therefore, is a glorious privilege of the men who fear the Lord. Alas, some of them are so lowly that they are not counted as worth taking notice of by the high ones of the world, but their betters respect them. The angels of God do not count themselves too good to attend on them, and camp about them to deliver them. This, then, is the man who has his angel wait upon him, even he who fears God.

7. Do you fear the Lord? Salvation is near you. "Surely His salvation is nigh them that fear Him, that glory may dwell in our land" (Psalm 85:9).

This is another privilege for those who fear the Lord. I told you before that the angel of the Lord encamped about them, but now it is said that His salvation is also near them. Although this does not altogether exclude the conduct of angels, but includes them, yet it looks further. Surely His salvation, His saving, pardoning grace, is near to those who fear Him, that is, to save them out of the hand of their spiritual enemies. The devil, sin, and death always wait to devour those who fear the Lord, but to deliver them from these His salvation attends them. So, then, if Satan tempts, their salvation is near; if sin, by breaking forth, beguiles them, here is God's salvation near them; yea, if death itself shall suddenly seize them, here is God's salvation near them.

8. Do you fear the Lord? Hearken yet again: "The mercy of the Lord is from everlasting to everlasting upon them that fear Him, and His righteousness unto children's children" (Psalm 103:17). This still confirms what was last asserted, that is, that His salvation is near them. But note this: there it is said that it is "*nigh* them," but here it is "*upon* them." His mercy is "upon them"; it covers them all over; it compasses them about as with a shield. Therefore they are said to be clothed with salvation, and covered with the robe of righteousness (Isaiah 61:10). The mercy of the Lord is upon them, to shelter and defend them. The mercy, the pardoning, preserving mercy, the mercy of the Lord, is upon them; who is he, then, who can condemn them?

But there yet is more. "The mercy of the Lord is from everlasting to everlasting upon them." It was designed for them before the world was, and shall be upon them when the world itself is ended. From everlasting to everlasting it is upon those who fear Him. This "from everlasting to everlasting" is that by which, in another place, the eternity of God Himself is declared. "From everlasting to everlasting, Thou art God" (Psalm 90:2). The meaning, then, may be this: so long as God has His being, so long shall the man who fears Him find mercy at His hand. According to Moses, "The eternal God is thy refuge, and underneath are the everlasting arms; and He shall thrust out the enemy from before thee, and shall say, 'Destroy them' " (Deuteronomy 33:27).

Child of God, you who fear God, here is mercy near you, mercy enough, everlasting mercy upon you. This is long-lived mercy. It will live longer than your sin; it will live longer than temptation; it will live longer than your sorrows; it will live longer than your persecutors. It is mercy *from* everlasting to contrive your salvation, and mercy *to* everlasting to weather it out with all your adversaries. Now, what can hell and death do to him who has this mercy of God upon him? And the man who fears the Lord has this.

Take that other blessed word and, you who fear the Lord, hang it like a chain of gold about your neck. "As the heaven is high above the earth, so great is His mercy toward them that fear Him" (Psalm 103:11). If mercy as big, as high, and as good as heaven itself will be a privilege, the man who fears God shall have such a privilege.

9. Do you fear God? "Like as a father pitieth his children, so the Lord pitieth them that fear Him" (Psalm 103:13).

"The Lord pitieth them that fear Him." He condoles and is affected, He feels and sympathizes with them in all their afflictions. It is a great matter for a poor man to be pitied in the affections of the great and mighty, but for a poor sinner to be thus in the heart and affections of God (and those who fear Him are so), this is astonishing to consider. "In all their affliction He was afflicted, and the angel of His presence saved them; in His love and in His pity He redeemed them; and He bore them, and carried them all the days of old" (Isaiah 63:9).

When it says that He pities them, it is as much as to say that He condoles, feels, and sympathizes with them in all their afflictions and temptations. So that this is the happiness of him who fears God: he has a God to pity him, and to be touched with all his miseries. It is said that "His soul was grieved for the misery of Israel" (Judges 10:16). And in Hebrews 4:15 He is said to be touched with the feeling of our infirmities, and can succor those who are tempted.

But further, let us take notice of the comparison. "As a father pitieth his children, so the Lord pitieth them that fear Him." Here is not only pity, but the pity of a relation, a father. It is said in Isaiah 49:15, "Can a woman [a mother] forget her sucking child, that she should not have compassion on the son of her womb? Yea, they may forget, yet will I not forget thee." The pity of neighbors and acquaintances helps in times of distress, but the pity of a father and a mother is a pity over and above that. "The Lord," says James 5:11, "is very pitiful, and of tender mercy." Pharaoh called Joseph his tender father because he provided for him against the famine; but how tender a father is God! How full of compassion, how full of pity! It is said that when Ephraim was afflicted, God's bowels were troubled for him, and turned within Him towards him. Oh, that the man who fears the Lord did but believe the pity and compassion that are in the heart of God and His Father towards him.

10. Do you fear God? "He will fulfill the desire of them that fear Him. He also will hear their cry, and will save them" (Psalm 145:19).

Almost all those places that make mention of the men who fear God speak as if they still were under affliction or in danger from an enemy. But here is still their privilege: their God is their Father, and He pities them.

"He will fulfill the desire of them that fear Him." Where, now, is the man who fears the Lord? Let him listen to this. What do you say, poor soul, will this content you? The Lord will fulfill your desires. It is intimated of Adonijah that David, his father, let him have his will in all things. "His father," says the text, "had not displeased him at any time in [so much as] saying, 'Why hast thou done so?' " (1 Kings 1:6). But here is more; here is a promise to grant you the whole desire of your heart, according to the prayer of holy David: the Lord "grant thee according to thine own heart, and fulfill all thy counsel. The Lord fulfill all thy petitions" (Psalm 20:4–5).

O you who fear the Lord, what is your desire? "All my desire," says David, "is all my salvation." So you say, "All my salvation is all my desire." Well, the desire of your soul is granted you. Yea, God Himself has engaged Himself to fulfill this desire. "He will fulfill the desire of them that fear Him. He also will hear their cry, and will save them." Oh, this desire, when it comes, what a tree of life will it be to you! You desire to be rid of your present trouble; the Lord shall rid you out of trouble. You desire to be delivered from temptation; the Lord shall deliver you out of temptation. You desire to be delivered from your body of death; and the Lord shall change your vile body that it may be like His glorious body (Philippians 3:21). You desire to be in the presence of God and among the angels in heaven. This desire shall also be fulfilled, and you shall be made equal to the angels. Oh, but it is a long way off! you say. Well, learn first to live upon your portion in the promise of it, and that will make your expectation of it sweet. God will fulfill your desires. God will do it. Though it tarries long, wait for it, because it will surely come; it will not tarry (Habakkuk 2:3).

11. Do you fear God? "The Lord taketh pleasure in them that fear Him" (Psalm 147:11). Those who fear God are among His chief delights. He delights in His Son. He delights in His works, and takes pleasure in those who fear Him. As a man takes pleasure in his wife, in his children, in his gold, and in his jewels, so the man who fears the Lord is the object of His delight. He takes pleasure in their prosperity, and therefore sends them health from the sanctuary, and makes them drink of the river of His pleasures. "They shall be abundantly satisfied with the fatness of Thy house; and Thou shalt make them drink of the river of Thy pleasures" (Psalm 36:8).

That or those we take pleasure in, we love to beautify and adorn with many ornaments. We count no cost too much to bestow on those in whom we place our delight, and whom we make the object of our pleasure. And so it is with God: "For the Lord taketh pleasure in His people." And what follows? "He will beautify the meek with salvation" (Psalm 149:4).

Those in whom we delight, we take pleasure in

their actions; yea, we teach them, and give them
such rules and laws to walk by as may yet make those
we love more pleasurable in our eyes. Therefore
those who fear God, since they are the objects of His
pleasure, are taught to know how to please Him in
everything. And hence it is said that He is ravished
with their looks, that He delights in their cry, and
that He is pleased with their walking.

Regarding those in whom we delight and take
pleasure, many things we will bear and put up with,
though they are not according to our minds. A man
will suffer or put up with that at the hand of the
child or wife of his pleasure that he will not pass by
nor put up with in another.

God, speaking of His people, says, " 'They shall
be Mine,' saith the Lord of hosts, 'in that day when I
make up My jewels; and I will spare them, as a man
spareth his own son that serveth him' " (Malachi
3:17).

Oh, how happy is the man who fears God! His
good thoughts, his good attempts to serve Him, and
his good life please God because he fears Him.

You know how pleasing the actions of our children are in our eyes when we know that they do what
they do from a reverential fear and awe of us. Yea,
though that which they do amounts but to little, we
take it well at their hands and are pleased therewith.
The woman who cast her two mites into the treasury
did not cast in much, for they made up but one farthing; yet how did the Lord Jesus trumpet her up!
He had pleasure in her and in her action. Therefore, that the Lord takes pleasure in those who fear
Him is another of their great privileges.

12. Do you fear God? The least portion of that fear gives the privilege of being blessed with the greatest saint. "He will bless them that fear the Lord, both small and great" (Psalm 115:13). This word "small" may be taken in three ways:

(1) By "small" sometimes is meant those who are small in esteem, those who are but little accounted of (Judges 6:15). Are you small or little in this sense? If you fear God you are sure to be blessed. "He will bless them that fear the Lord, both small and great." Be you never so small in the world's eyes, in your own eyes, or in the saints' eyes (as sometimes one saint is little in another saint's eye), yet because you fear God you are put among the blessed.

(2) By "small" sometimes is meant those who are but small in stature or young in years, little children who are easily passed by and looked over, as those who sang hosanna in the temple were when the Pharisees deridingly said of them to Christ, "Hearest Thou what these say?" (Matthew 21:16). Well, but Christ would not despise those children who feared God, but actually preferred them, by the Scripture testimony, far before those who condemned them. Little children, however small, and although of never so small esteem with men, shall also, if they fear the Lord, be blessed with the greatest saints. "He will bless them that fear the Lord, both small and great."

(3) By "small" may sometimes be meant those who are small in grace or gifts. These are said to be the least in the church, that is, under this consideration, and so are by it least esteemed. Thus also is that word of Christ to be understood, "Inasmuch as

ye did it not to one of the least of these, ye did it not to Me" (Matthew 25:45).

Are you, in your own thoughts or in the thoughts of others, one of these small ones? Small in grace, small in gifts, small in esteem upon this account? Yet if you fear God, if you fear God indeed, you are certainly blessed with the best of saints. The least star stands as fixed as the biggest of them all in heaven. "He shall bless them that fear Him, both small and great." He shall bless them, that is, with the same blessing of eternal life; for the different degrees of grace in saints do not make the blessing, as to its nature, differ. It is the same heaven, the same life, the same glory, and the same eternity of felicity that they are promised to be blessed with in this text. That truth is observable in the passage which I mentioned before, where Christ, at the day of judgment, particularly mentions and owns the least: "Inasmuch as ye did it not to one of the least." The least, then, were there in His kingdom and in His glory as well as the biggest of all.

"He shall bless them that fear Him, both small and great." The small are named first in the text, and are thus first in rank, perhaps to show that though they may be slighted and little valued in the world, yet they are much valued in the eyes of the Lord.

Are only great saints to have the kingdom and the glory everlasting? Are only great works to be rewarded, works that are done by virtue of great grace and the abundance of the gifts of the Holy Ghost? No, "Whosoever shall give to drink unto one of these little ones a cup of cold water only in the name of a disciple, verily I say unto you, he shall in no wise lose his reward" (Matthew 10:42). Mark, here is but a little gift, a cup of cold water, and that given to a little saint; but both are taken special notice of by our Lord Jesus Christ. He will give reward to His servants, the prophets, and to His saints, and to those who fear His name, both small and great (Revelation 11:18).

The small, therefore, among those who fear God, are blessed with the great (and as much as the great) with the same salvation, the same glory, and the same eternal life; and they shall have, even as the great ones also shall have, as much as they can carry, as much as their hearts, souls, bodies and capacities can hold.

13. Do you fear God? Why, the Holy Ghost has purposely dictated for you a whole psalm to sing concerning yourself, so that you may, even as you are in your calling, bed, journey, or wherever, sing out your own blessed and happy condition to your own comfort, and the comfort of your fellows. I will set out Psalm 128 before you:

> Blessed is everyone that feareth the Lord, that walketh in His ways. For thou shalt eat the labor of thine hands; happy shalt thou be, and it shall be well with thee. Thy wife shall be as a fruitful vine by the sides of thine house, thy children like olive plants round about thy table. Behold that thus shall the man be blessed that feareth the Lord. The Lord shall bless thee out of Zion, and thou shalt see the good of Jerusalem all the days of thy life. Yea, thou shalt see thy children's children, and peace upon Israel.

I will be done with the privileges once I remove this one objection.

OBJECTION. But the Scripture says, "Perfect love casteth out fear" (1 John 4:18); and therefore it seems that saints, after the Spirit of adoption has come, should not fear, but do their duty, as another Scripture says, "without fear" (Luke 1:74).

ANSWER. Fear, as I have shown you, may be taken in several ways:

It may be taken for the fear of devils.

It may be taken for the fear of reprobates.

It may be taken for the fear that is wrought in the godly by the Spirit as the Spirit of bondage.

Or it may be taken for the fear of which I have been discoursing.

Now the fear that perfect love casts out cannot be that sonlike, gracious fear of God that I have in this last place been treating, because that fear which love casts out gives torments, but the sonlike fear does not. Therefore, the fear which love casts out is either that which is of devils and reprobates, or that which is begotten in the heart by the Spirit of God as a Spirit of bondage, or both. For, indeed, all these kinds of fear have torment, and therefore may be cast out, and are so by the Spirit of adoption, which is called the Spirit of faith and love, when He comes with power into the soul. So without this fear we should serve Him.

But to argue from these texts that we ought not to fear God, or to mix fear with our worship of Him, is as much as to say that by the Spirit of adoption we are brought under condemnation, for he who does not fear God is in such a state. But what I have affirmed the Scripture plentifully confirms, saying, "Happy is the man that feareth alway" (Proverbs 28:14). And again, "It shall be well with them that fear God, which fear before Him" (Ecclesiastes 8:12).

The fear of the Lord, therefore, is a grace that greatly beautifies a Christian, his words, and all his ways. "Wherefore now let the fear of the Lord be upon you; take heed and do it, for there is no iniquity with the Lord our God, nor respect of persons, nor taking of gifts" (2 Chronicles 19:7).

Chapter 6

The Use of This Doctrine

Having proceeded this far about this doctrine of the fear of God, I now come to make some use and application of the whole.

USE OF EXAMINATION. Is this fear of God such an excellent thing? Is it attended with so many blessed privileges? Then this should put every one of us upon a diligent examination of ourselves, namely whether this grace is in us or not. For if it is, then you are one of these blessed ones to whom belong these glorious privileges, for you have an interest in every one of them. But if it shall appear that this grace is not in you, then your state is fearfully miserable, as has partly been manifested already, and will further be seen in what comes after.

Now, the better to help you to consider, and not to miss in finding out, what you are in your self-examination, I will speak to this both in general and in particular.

In general. No man brings this grace into the world with him. Everyone by nature is destitute of it, for naturally none fear God. "There is no fear of God," none of this grace of fear, "before their eyes" (Romans 3:18). They do not so much as know what it is; for this fear flows, as was shown before, from a new heart, faith, repentance, and the like. If you are devoid of this new heart, faith, and repentance you are also devoid of this godly fear. Men must have a

122

mighty change of heart and life or else they are
strangers to this fear of God. Alas, how ignorant are
most of this! Yea, and some are not afraid to say they
are not changed, nor desire so to be. Can these fear
God? Can these be possessed with this grace of fear?
No! "Because they have no changes, therefore they
fear not God" (Psalm 55:19).

Wherefore, sinner, consider, whoever you are
who are destitute of this fear of God, that you are devoid of all other graces; for this fear, as I have
shown, flows from the whole stock of grace where it
is present. There is not one of the graces of the
Spirit but this fear is in it; yea, as I may say, this fear
is the flower and beauty of every grace; neither is
there anything, let it look as much like grace as it
will, that will be counted so indeed if the fruit
thereof is not this fear of God. Wherefore, I say
again, consider well this matter, for as you shall be
found with reference to this grace, so shall your
judgment be. I have but briefly treated this grace
above, yet have endeavored with words as fit as I
could to display it in its colors before your face—
first by showing you what this fear of God is, then
what it flows from, as also what flows from it. To
this, as was said before, I have added several privileges that are annexed to this fear, that by all, if it
may be, you may recognize it if you have it, and see
you are without it if you do not have it. I refer you
back to the previous chapters for these points.

In particular. I conclude with these various propositions concerning those who do not fear God.

1. The man who is proud and of a high and lofty
mind does not fear God. This is plain from the

exhortation of Romans 11:20: "Be not high minded, but fear." Here you see that a high mind and the fear of God are set in direct opposition one to the other, and the apostle concludes that they cannot be present together: where there is a high mind there is not the fear of God, and where there is the fear of God, the mind is not high, but lowly. Can a man at the same time be a proud man and fear God too? Why, then, is it said that God beholds everyone who is proud and abases him, and that He beholds the proud afar off (Job 40:11; Psalm 138:6)?

He, therefore, who is proud of his person, of his riches, of his office, of his parts and the like, does not fear God. This point is also manifest further, for "God resisteth the proud" (James 4:6), which He would not do if he feared Him. But in that He sets him at such a distance from Him, in that He testifies that He will abase him and resist him, it is evident that he is not the man who has this grace of fear; for that man, as I have shown you, is the man of God's delight, the object of His pleasure.

2. The covetous man does not fear God. This also is plain from the Word, because it sets covetousness and the fear of God in direct opposition. Men who fear God are said to hate covetousness (Exodus 18:21). Besides, the covetous man is called an idolater, and is said to have no part in the kingdom of Christ and of God (Colossians 3:5). And "The wicked boasteth of his heart's desire, and blesseth the covetous, whom the Lord abhorreth" (Psalm 10:3).

Hearken to this, you who hunt the world to take it, you who care not how you get, so long as you get the world. You who make even religion your stalking horse to get the world do fear not God. And what will you do, whose hearts follow after your covetousness; you who are led by covetousness up and down, as it were, by the nose, sometimes to swear, to lie, to deceive, cheat, and defraud, when you can gain an advantage by so doing? You are far, very far from the fear of God. "Ye adulterers and adulteresses" (for so the covetous are called), "know ye not that the friendship of the world is enmity with God? Whosoever therefore will be a friend of the world is the enemy of God" (James 4:4).

3. The riotous eaters of flesh have not the fear of God; for this is done without fear (Jude 12). Gluttony is a sin little taken notice of, and as little repented of by those who commit it; yet it is odious in the sight of God, and the practice of it is a demonstration of the want of His fear in the heart. Yea, so odious is it that God forbids that His people should so much as keep company with such. "Be not," says He, "among wine-bibbers, among riotous eaters of flesh" (Proverbs 23:20). And He further tells us that those who are such are spots and blemishes to those who keep them company, for indeed they fear not God (2 Peter 2:13).

Alas, some men are as if they were born for nothing else but to eat, drink, and pamper their carcasses with the dainties of this world, quite forgetting why God sent them here! But such fear not God, and so, consequently, are of the number of those upon whom the day of judgment will come unawares (Luke 21:34).

4. The liar is one who fears not God. This also is evident from Isaiah 57:11: "Thou hast lied, and hast

not remembered Me, nor laid it to thy heart; have
not I held My peace even of old, and thou fearest Me
not?" What lie this was is not material; it was a lie, or
a course of lying, that is here rebuked, and the person or persons in this practice were such as feared
not God. A course of lying and the fear of God cannot stand together.

This sin of lying is a common sin, and it walks in
the world in several disguises. There is the profane,
scoffing liar; there is the cunning, artificial liar;
there is the hypocritical, religious liar; there are
liars of other ranks and degrees. But none of them
have the fear of God, nor shall any of them, unless
they repent, escape the damnation of hell. "All liars
shall have their part in the lake which burneth with
fire and brimstone" (Revelation 21:8). Heaven and
the new Jerusalem are not a place for such: "And
there shall in no wise enter into it anything that de-
fileth, neither whatsoever worketh abomination, or
maketh a lie" (verse 27). Therefore Revelation 22:15
says, "Without are dogs, and sorcerers, and whore-
mongers, and murderers, and idolaters, and whosoever loveth and maketh a lie." But this would not be
their sentence, judgment, and condemnation if
those who are liars were such as had in them this
blessed fear of God.

5. Those fear not God who cry unto Him for help
in the time of their calamity and, when they are delivered, return to their former rebellion. Moses, in a
spirit of prophecy, asserts this at the time of the
mighty judgment of the hail. Pharaoh then desired
him to pray to God that He would take that judgment away from him. "Well, so I will," said Moses,

"but as for thee and thy servants, I know that ye will not fear the Lord God" (Exodus 9:30). It is as if he had said, "I know that as soon as this judgment is removed, you will go to your old rebellion again." And what greater demonstration can be given that such a man fears not God than to cry to God to be delivered from affliction to prosperity, and to spend that prosperity in rebellion against Him? This is crying for mercies so that they may be spent (or that we may have something to spend) upon our lusts and in the service of Satan (James 4:3). Of these God complains in Ezekiel 16:17: "Thou hast also taken thy fair jewels of My gold and of My silver, which I had given thee, and madest to thyself images of men, and didst commit whoredom with them."

This was for want of the fear of God. Many of this kind there are now in the world, men, women, and children alike. Are not you who reads this book of this number? Have you not cried for health when sick, for wealth when poor, when lame for strength, when in prison for liberty, and then spent all that you got by your prayer in the service of Satan and to gratify your lusts? Look to it, sinner, these things are signs that you fear not God with your heart.

6. Those fear not God who waylay His people, and seek to overthrow them or to turn them aside from the right path as they are journeying from here to their eternal rest. This is evident from Deuteronomy 25:17–18: "Remember what Amalek did unto thee by the way, when ye were come forth out of Egypt; how he met thee by the way, and smote the hindmost of thee, even all that were feeble behind thee, when thou wast faint and weary; and he feared not God."

Many such Amalekites there are now in the world, who have set themselves against the feeble of the flock especially, still smiting them, some by power, some with the tongue, some in their lives and estates, some in their names and reputations, by scandal, slanders, and reproach. But the reason for this ungodly practice is that they fear not God; for if they feared Him they would be afraid to so much as think—much less attempt—to afflict and destroy and calumniate the children of God. But such there have been, such there are, and such there will be in the world, for not all men fear God.

7. Those fear not God who see His hand upon backsliders for their sins, and yet themselves will be backsliders also. "I saw," says God, "when for all the causes whereby backsliding Israel committed adultery I had put her away and given her a bill of divorce, yet her treacherous sister Judah feared not, but went and played the harlot also" (Jeremiah 3:8).

Judah saw that her sister was put away and delivered by God into the hand of Shalmanezer, who carried her away beyond Babylon; and yet, though she saw it, she went and played the harlot also, a sign of great hardness of heart, and of the want of the fear of God indeed. Had His fear been in her heart, it would have taught her to tremble at the judgment executed upon her sister, and not to have gone and played the harlot also—not to have done it while her sister's judgment was in sight and memory. But what is it that a heart destitute of the fear of God will not do? No sin comes amiss to such; yea, they will sin; they will do that themselves, for the doing of which they believe some are in hellfire, and all because they fear not God.

But observe, if those who take no warning when they see the hand of God upon backsliders are said to have none of the fear of God, do those have it, do you think, who lay stumbling blocks in the way of God's people and use devices to cause them to backslide, yea, who rejoice when they can do this mischief to any? And yet there are many of this sort in the world, who even rejoice when they see a professor fall into sin and go back from his profession, as if they had found some excellent thing.

8. Those fear not God who can look upon a land wallowing in sin, and yet are not humbled at the sight thereof. "Have ye forgotten," said God by the prophet to the Jews, "the wickedness of your fathers, and the wickedness of the kings of Judah, and the wickedness of their wives, and your own wickedness, and the wickedness of your wives, which they have committed in the land of Judah, and in the streets of Jerusalem? They are not humbled even unto this day, neither have they feared nor walked in My law" (Jeremiah 44:9–10).

Here was a land full of wickedness, and none to bewail it; for they wanted the fear of God. If those who are not humbled at their own and others' wickedness are said not to fear or have the fear of God, what shall we think or say of those who receive, who nourish and rejoice in such wickedness? Do they fear God? Yea, what shall we say of those who are the inventors and promoters of wickedness, as of oaths, beastly talk, or the like? Do you think they fear God?

Once again, what shall we say of those who cannot be content to be wicked themselves, and to invent and rejoice in other men's wickedness, but must hate, reproach, vilify, and abuse those whom they cannot persuade to be wicked? Do they fear God?

9. Those who take more heed to their own dreams than to the Word of God fear not God. This also is plain from Ecclesiastes 5:7: "For in the multitude of dreams and many words there are also divers vanities; but fear thou God"; that is, take heed to His Word.

Here the fear of God is opposed to our overly heeding dreams, and it is implied that it is for want of the fear of God that men so greatly heed those things.

What will those say to this who give more heed to a suggestion which arises from their foolish hearts, or that is cast in there by the devil, than they do to the holy Word of God? These are "filthy dreamers" (Jude 8).

Also, what shall we say to those who are more confident of the mercy of God to their souls, because He has blessed them with outward things, than they are afraid of His wrath and condemnation, though the whole of the Word of God fully verifies the same? These are filthy dreamers indeed.

A dream is either real, or so by way of semblance; and so some men dream sleeping and some waking. And as those that a man dreams sleeping are caused either by God, Satan, business, the flesh, or the like, so are those that a man dreams while awake, sometimes to divert our minds from those that we have in our sleep.

When awake in the body, men may have dreams, that is, visions from heaven, which have a tendency to reveal to the sinner his state, or the state of the Church according to the Word.

But those that are from Satan, business, and the flesh are such (especially the first and last, namely from Satan and the flesh) as tend to embolden men to hope for good in a way disagreeing with the Word of God. These Jude calls "filthy dreamers," such whose principles were their dreams, and led them to defile the flesh, that is, by fornication and uncleanness; to "despise dominion" that the reins might be laid upon the neck of their lusts; to "speak evil of dignities," of those whom God had set over them to govern them in all the law and testament of Christ. These dreamed that to live like brutes, to be greedy of gain, and to take away for it, as Cain and Balaam did by their wiles, the lives of the owners thereof, would go for good coin in the best of trials. These also Peter speaks of in 2 Peter 2. And he describes their dreams, as Jude calls them, as their principles and errors in life and doctrine. You may read of them in that whole chapter where they are called "cursed children" (verse 14), and so, by consequence, such as fear not God.

10. Those fear not God who are sorcerers, adulterers, false swearers, and who deprive the hireling of his wages.

It is a custom with some men to keep back by fraud from the hireling that which by covenant they agreed to pay for their labor—pinching, I say, and paring from them their due which of right belongs to them, to make them cry in the ears of the Lord of

Sabaoth (James 5:4). These fear not God; they are
reckoned among the worst of men, and in their day
of account God Himself will bear witness against
them. " 'And I will come near to you to judgment;
and I will be a swift witness against the sorcerers,
and against the adulterers, and against false swearers, and against those that oppress the hireling in
his wages, the widow, and the fatherless, and that
turn aside the stranger from his right, and fear not
Me,' saith the Lord" (Malachi 3:5).

11. Those fear not God who, instead of pitying,
rail at God's people in their afflictions, temptations,
and persecutions, and rather rejoice and skip for joy
than sympathize with them in their sorrow. Thus
did David's enemies; thus did Israel's enemies; and
thus did the thief: he railed at Christ when He hung
upon the cross, and was for that, even by his fellow,
accounted as one who feared not God (Luke 23:40).

It is a common thing among the children of
men to rejoice at the hurt of those who fear God,
and it arises from an inward hatred of godliness.
"They hate you," says Christ, "because they hated
Me" (John 15:18). Therefore Christ takes what is
done to His people in this world as done to Himself,
and so as a sign of holiness of life.

But this falls hard upon such as despise and rejoice to see God's people in their griefs, and who
take the opportunity, as dogged Shimei did, to aug-
ment the griefs and afflictions of God's people
(2 Samuel 16:5–8).

12. Those fear not God who are strangers to the
effects of fear. "If I be a Master, where is My fear?"
(Malachi 1:6). That is, show that I am so by your fear

of Me, and in the effects of your fear of Me. "You offer polluted bread upon Mine altar" (verse 7). This is not a sign that you fear God. You offer the blind for sacrifices, where is My fear? You offer the lame and the sick; these are not effects of the fear of God (verse 8).

Sinner, it is one thing to say, "I fear God," and another to fear Him indeed. Therefore James says, "I will show thee my faith by my works" (James 2:18), and here God calls for a testimony of your fear by the effects of fear. I have already shown you several effects of fear. If you are a stranger to them, you are a stranger to this grace of fear. Therefore, to conclude this, it is not a feigned profession that will do; nothing is good here but what is salted with this fear of God. And those who fear Him are men of truth, men of singleness of heart, perfect, upright, humble, holy men. Wherefore, reader, examine, and again I say, examine yourself. Lay the Word and your heart together before you conclude that you fear God.

What? Fear God and remain in a state of nature? Fear God without a change of heart and life? What? Fear God, and be proud and covetous, a wine-bibber, and a riotous eater of flesh? Fear God and be a liar, and one who cries for mercies to spend them upon your lusts? This would be strange!

True, you may fear as devils do, but what will that profit? You may, by your fear, be driven away from God, from His worship, people, and ways; but what will that avail? It may be that you so fear at present as to be a little stopped in your sinful course. Perhaps you have gotten a reproof from the Word of God, and are at present a little hindered from your former and full career after sin. But what of that? If by the fear that you have your heart is not united to God, and to the love of His Son, Word, and people, your fear is worth nothing.

Many men also are forced to fear God the same as underlings are forced to fear those who are above them by force. If you only thus fear God, it is but a false fear; it flows not from love of God. This fear brings not willing subjection, which indeed brings the effect of right fear; but being overpowered, like a hypocrite, you subject yourself by feigned obedience, being forced, I say, by mere dread to do it (Psalm 66:3).

It is said, "The fame of David went out into all lands; and the Lord brought the fear of him upon all nations" (1 Chronicles 14:17). But did they now love David? Did they now choose him to be their king? No, verily; many of them rather hated him, and, when they could, made resistance against him. They did even as you do: they feared, but did not love; they feared him, but did not choose his government to rule over them.

It is also said of Jehoshaphat, when God had subdued before him Ammon, Moab, and Mount Seir, that "the fear of God was on all the kingdoms of those countries, when they heard that the Lord fought against the enemies of Israel" (2 Chronicles 20:29). But, I say, was this fear that is called here "the fear of God" anything else but a dread of the greatness and power of the king? No, verily, nor did that dread bring them into a willing subjection to and liking of His laws and government. It only made them, like slaves and underlings, stand in fear of

His executing the vengeance of God upon them.

Therefore, notwithstanding this fear, they were rebels to Him in their hearts; and, when occasion and advantage offered themselves, they showed it by rising in rebellion against Israel.

This fear, therefore, provoked but feigned and forced obedience, a right emblem of the obedience of such who, being still enemies in their minds to God, are forced, by virtue of present conviction, to yield a little, even of fear, to God, to His Word, and to His ordinances. Reader, whoever you are, think of this: it is your concern, therefore do it. Examine, and examine again, and look diligently to your heart in your examination so that it does not beguile you about so great a concern as indeed the fear of God is.

Let me warn you of one thing more before I leave you. Take heed of deferring to fear the Lord. Some men, when they have had conviction upon their heart that the fear of God is not in them, have, through the overpowering of their corruptions, yet deferred and put off the fear of God from them, as it is said of those in Jeremiah: "This people hath a revolting and rebellious heart; they are revolted and gone; neither say they in their heart, 'Let us now fear the Lord' " (Jeremiah 5:23–24). They saw that the judgments of God attended them because they did not yet fear God; but that conviction would not prevail with them to say, "Let us now fear the Lord." They were for deferring to fear Him still; they were for putting off His fear from them longer.

Sinner, have you deferred to fear the Lord? Is your heart still so stubborn as not yet to say, "Let us fear the Lord"? Oh, the Lord has taken notice of your rebellion, and is preparing some dreadful judgment for you! " 'Shall I not visit for these things?' saith the Lord. 'Shall not My soul be avenged on such a nation as this' " (verse 29)?

Sinner, why should you pull vengeance down from heaven upon yourself? Look up. Perhaps you have already been pulling this great while, to pull it down upon you. Oh, pull no longer! Why be your own executioner? Fall down upon your knees, man, and lift up your heart and your hands to the God who dwells in the heavens. Cry, yea, cry aloud, "Lord, unite my heart to fear Thy name, and do not harden my heart from Thy fear." Thus holy men have cried before you, and by crying have prevented judgment.

Before I leave this use, let me give you a few things that, if God will, may provoke you to fear the Lord.

The man who fears not God carries it worse toward himself than the brute beast carries it towards that man. "The fear of you and the dread of you shall be upon every beast of the earth, and upon every fowl of the air, upon all that moveth upon the earth, and upon all the fishes in the sea" (Genesis 9:2).

Mark, "All My creatures shall fear you and dread you," says God. "None of them shall be so hardy as to cast off all reverence of you." But what a shame is it to man that God should subject all His creatures to him, and he should refuse to stoop his heart to God! The beast, the bird, the fish, and all have a fear and dread of men, which God has placed in their hearts, yet man is devoid of godly fear, of Him who thus lovingly has put all things under him. Sinner! Are you

not ashamed that a silly cow, a sheep, and even
swine should better observe the law of creation than
you do the law of your God?

Consider, he who will not fear God, God will
make him fear Him whether he will or not. That is,
he who does not, who will not now so fear Him as
willingly to bow before Him and put his neck into
His yoke, God will make him fear Him when He
comes to take vengeance on him. Then He will sur-
round him with terror and fear on every side: fear
within and fear without; fear shall be in the way,
even in the way that you go when you are going out
of this world; and that will be dreadful fear. God
says, "I will choose their delusions, and will bring
their fears upon them" (Isaiah 66:4).

He who fears not God now, the Lord shall laugh
at his fears then. Sinner, God will get even with
those who choose not to have His fear in their
hearts; for as He calls and they hear not now, so they
shall cry, yea howl then, and He will laugh at their
fears. "I will laugh," He says, "at your calamity. I will
mock when your fear cometh; when your fear
cometh as desolation, and your destruction cometh
as a whirlwind; when distress and anguish cometh
upon you. Then shall they call upon Me, but I will
not answer; they shall seek Me early, but they shall
not find Me. For they hated knowledge, and did not
choose the fear of the Lord" (Proverbs 1:26–29).

Sinner! You think to escape the fear, but what
will you do with the pit? You think to escape the pit,
but what will you do with the snare? "The snare," you
say, "what is that?" I answer, it is the work of your
own hands. "The wicked is snared in the work of his

own hands" (Psalm 9:16). "The wicked is snared by the transgression of his lips" (Proverbs 12:13).

Sinner! What will you do when you come into this snare, that is, into the guilt and terror that your sins will bind you with when they, like a cord, are fastened about your soul? This snare will bring you back again to the pit, which is hell; and then what will you do to be rid of your fear? The fear, pit, and snare shall come upon you because you fear not God.

Sinner! Are you one of those who have cast off fear? Poor man, what will you do when these three things beset you? Where will you flee for help, and where will you leave your glory? If you flee from the fear, there is the pit; if you flee from the pit, there is the snare.

USE OF EXHORTATION. My next word shall be an exhortation to saints to fear God. "Oh, fear the Lord, ye His saints; for there is no want to them that fear Him" (Psalm 34:9).

Not but that every saint does fear God; but, as the apostle says in another case, "I beseech you that ye would abound more and more" (1 Thessalonians 4:1). The fear of the Lord, as I have shown you, is a grace of the new covenant, as other saving graces are, and so is capable of being stronger or weaker, as other graces are. Wherefore, I beseech you, fear Him more and more.

It is said of Obadiah that "he feared the Lord greatly." Every saint fears the Lord, but every saint does not *greatly* fear Him. Oh, there are but few Obadiahs in the world (I mean among the saints on earth)! See the whole description of him in 1 Kings 18. As Paul said of Timothy, "I have no man like-minded" (Philippians 2:20), so it may be said of some concerning the fear of the Lord: they have scarcely an equal. So it was with Job: "There is none like him in the earth, a perfect and an upright man, one that feareth God and escheweth evil" (Job 1:8). There was no one in Job's day who feared God like him; no, there was not one like him in all the earth. Surely there were others in the world who feared God; but this fearing of Him *greatly* is the thing that saints should do, and that was the thing that Job did—and in that he outstripped his fellows.

It is also said that Hananiah "was a faithful man, and feared God above many" (Nehemiah 7:2). He also had gotten, as to the exercise of and growth in this grace, beyond many of his brethren. He "feared God above many." Now, then, seeing this grace admits of degrees, and is in some stronger and in some weaker, let us be all awakened, as to other graces, so to this grace also, so that as you "abound in everything, in faith, and utterance, and knowledge, and in all diligence, and in your love to us, see that ye abound in this grace also" (2 Corinthians 8:7).

I will labor to enforce this exhortation upon you by several motives.

Motives to Fear God

1. Let God's distinguishing love for you be a motive to you to fear Him greatly. He has put His fear in your heart, and has not given that blessing to your

neighbor, perhaps not to your husband, your wife, your child, or your parent. Oh, what an obligation should this thought lay upon your heart to greatly fear the Lord! Remember also that this fear of the Lord is His treasure, a choice jewel, given only to favorites, and to those who are greatly beloved.

Great gifts naturally tend to oblige, and will do so, I trust, with you when you shall ingenuously consider it. It is a sign of a very bad nature when the contrary shows itself. Could God have done more for you than to have put His fear in your heart? This is better than to have given you a place in heaven without it. Yea, had He given you all faith, all knowledge, the tongue of men and angels, and a place in heaven to boot, they would all have been short of this gift of the fear of God in your heart. Therefore love it, nourish it, exercise it; use all means to cause it to increase and grow in your heart so that it may appear that it is always in your mind, poor sinner.

2. Another motive to stir you up to grow in this grace of the fear of God may be the privileges that it puts you under. Where will you find in the Bible so many privileges so affectionately entailed to any grace as to the fear of God? God speaks of this grace, and of the privileges that belong to it, as if (to speak with reverence) He did not know how to stop blessing the man who has it.

It seems to me that this grace of fear is the darling grace, the grace that God sets His heart upon to the highest degree. As it were, He embraces and lays the man in His bosom who possesses and grows strong in this grace of the fear of God.

See again the many privileges in which that man

has an interest who has this grace in his heart; and
see also that few of them are mentioned without the
pronunciation of a blessing being linked to them,
or else that man is spoken of by way of admiration.

3. Another motive may be this: the man who
grows in this grace of the fear of the Lord will escape those evils into which others will fall. Where
this grace is, it keeps the soul from final apostasy. "I
will put My fear in their hearts, that they shall not
depart from Me" (Jeremiah 32:40). Yet if there is not
an increase in this grace, much evil may attend and
be committed notwithstanding.

There is a child who is healthy, and has its limbs,
and can walk, but it is careless. Now, the evil of carelessness disadvantages it greatly. Carelessness is the
reason why that child stumbles or falls into the dirt,
yea, why sometimes it is burned or nearly drowned.
Thus it is even with God's people who fear Him: because they do not add to their fear a concern for
growing more in the fear of God, therefore they reap
damage; whereas, were they more in His fear, it
would keep them better, deliver them more, and
preserve them from these snares of death.

4. Another motive may be this: to grow in this
grace of the fear of God is the way to be kept always
in a conscientious performance of Christian duties.
An increase in this grace, I say, keeps every grace in
exercise, and the keeping of our graces in their due
exercise produces a conscientious performance of
duties.

You have a watch, perhaps, in your pocket, but
the hand may not as yet be kept in any good order,
but always lies to you as to the hour of the day. The

way to remedy this is but to look well to the spring and the wheels within; for if they go right, so will the hand also.

This is your case in spiritual things. You are a gracious man, and the fear of God is in you; yet, for all that, one cannot well tell by your life what time of day it is. You give no true and constant sign that you are indeed a Christian. The reason is that you do not look well to this grace of the fear of God; you do not grow and increase in that, but suffer your heart to grow careless and hard, and so your life grows remiss and worldly. Job's growing great in the fear of God made him flee evil.

5. This is the way to be wise indeed. "A wise man feareth, and departeth from evil" (Proverbs 14:16). It does not say a wise man has the grace of fear, but a wise man fears; that is, he puts this grace into exercise. There is no greater sign of wisdom than to grow in this blessed grace. Is it not a sign of wisdom to depart from sins which are the snares of death and hell? Is it not a sign of wisdom for a man yet more and more to endeavor to gain an interest in the love and protection of God? Is it not a high point of wisdom for a man to be always doing that which conforms him to the conduct of angels? Surely this is wisdom! And if it is a blessing to have this fear, is it not wisdom to increase in it? Doubtless it is the highest point of wisdom, as I have shown before; therefore grow therein.

6. It is seemly for saints to fear, and increase in the fear of God.

He is your Creator. And is it not seemly for creatures to fear and reverence their Creator? He is your

King. Is it not seemly for subjects to fear and reverence their king? He is your Father. Is it not seemly
for children to reverence and fear their father? Yea,
and to do it more and more?

7. It is honorable to grow in this grace of fear.
"When Ephraim spake trembling, he exalted himself in Israel" (Hosea 13:1).

Truly to fear, and to abound in this fear, is a sign
of a very princely spirit; and the reason is that when
I greatly fear my God I am above the fear of all others, nor can anything in this world, be it never so
terrible and dreadful, move me at all to fear them.
And hence it is that Christ counsels us to fear: "And
I say unto you, my friends, be not afraid of them that
kill the body, and after that have no more that they
can do. But I will forewarn you whom ye shall fear:
fear Him, which after He hath killed hath power to
cast into hell; yea, I say unto you, fear Him" (Luke
12:4–5).

Indeed, this true fear of God sets a man above all
the world; and therefore it is said again, "Neither
fear ye their fear, nor be afraid. Sanctify the Lord of
hosts Himself; and let Him be your fear, and let Him
be your dread" (Isaiah 8:12–13).

Ranting boasters who are ignorant of the nature
of the fear of God count it a poor, sneaking, pitiful,
cowardly spirit in men to fear and tremble before
the Lord; but whosoever looks back to jails, and gib-
bets, to the sword and burning stake, shall see that
there has been seen the most mighty and invincible
spirit that has been in the world.

Yea, see if God does not consider that the growth
of His people in this grace of fear is that which

makes them honorable, when He excludes those
from a dwelling place in His house who do not
honor them who fear Him. And He says, moreover,
"A woman that feareth the Lord, she shall be
praised" (Proverbs 31:30). If the world and godless
men will not honor these, they shall be honored in
some other way. "Them," He says, "that honor Me, I
will honor" (1 Samuel 2:30); and they shall be honored in heaven, in the churches, and among angels.

8. This fear, and its increase, qualifies a man to
be entrusted with heavenly and spiritual things, yea,
and with earthly things too.

With heavenly and spiritual things. "My covenant,"
says God, "was with him of life and peace; and I gave
them to him for the fear wherewith he feared Me,
and was afraid before My name" (Malachi 2:5).
Behold what a gift, what a mercy, what a blessing
this Levi is entrusted with, namely with God's everlasting covenant, and with the life and peace that
are wrapped up in this covenant! But why is it given
to him? The answer is, "For the fear wherewith he
feared Me, and was afraid before My name." And the
reason is good; for this fear of God teaches man to
put a due estimate upon every gift of God bestowed
upon us. Also it teaches us to make use of these gifts
with reverence for His name, and respect of His
glory in most godly wisdom, all which becomes him
who is entrusted with any spiritual gift. The gift here
was given to Levi to minister to his brethren doctri-
nally thereof, "for he," says God, "shall teach Jacob
My statutes and Israel My law" (Deuteronomy 33:10).

See also Exodus 18:21 and Nehemiah 7:2, along
with many other places that might be named, and

you will find that men fearing God and hating covetousness, men who fear God above others, are entrusted by God, yea, and by His Church too, with the trust and administration of spiritual things before any other in the world.

With earthly things. The fear of God qualifies a man to be entrusted with these also rather than with another. Therefore God made Joseph lord of all Egypt; Obadiah, steward of Ahab's house; Daniel, Mordecai, and the three children were set over the province of Babylon, and this by the wonderfully working hand of God, because He wished to dispose of earthly things now not only in a common way, but for the good of His people in particular. True, when there is no special thing to be done by God in a nation for His people, then whosoever will, that is, whether they have grace or not, may have the disposal of those things; but if God has anything special to bestow upon His people of this world's goods, then He will entrust it to the hands of men fearing God. Joseph must now be made lord of Egypt because Israel must be kept from starving; Obadiah must now be made steward of Ahab's house because the Lord's prophets must be hidden from and fed in spite of the rage and cruel mind of Jezebel. Daniel, with his companions, and Mordecai also, were exalted to earthly and temporal dignity so that they might in that state, they being men who abounded in the fear of God, be serviceable to their brethren in their straits and difficulties.

9. Where the fear of God in the heart of any is not growing, no grace thrives, nor is duty done as it should be.

There no grace thrives—neither faith, hope, love, nor any grace. This is evident from that general exhortation: "Let us cleanse ourselves from all filthiness of the flesh and spirit, perfecting holiness in the fear of God" (2 Corinthians 7:1). Perfecting holiness, what is that? But as James says of patience, let every grace have its "perfect work, that ye may be perfect and entire, wanting nothing" (James 1:4).

But this cannot be done but in the fear of God, yea, in the exercise of that grace, and so, consequently, in the growth of it; for there is no grace but grows, if it is exercised. If then you would be perfect in holiness, if you would have every grace that God has put into your souls grow and flourish unto perfection, lay them to soak in this grace of fear, and do all in the exercise of it; for "a little done in the fear of the Lord is better than the revenues of the wicked" (Proverbs 16:8). Again, the Lord will not suffer the soul of the righteous, the soul that lives in the fear of the Lord, to famish; but He casts away the abundance of the wicked. Bring your abundance to God, and if it is not seasoned with godly fear, it shall not be acceptable to Him, but loathsome and abominable in His sight; for it does not flow from the spirit of the fear of the Lord.

Therefore, where there is not a growth in this fear, no duty is done acceptably. This flows from that which goes before, for if grace rather decays than grows, where this grace of fear is not growing and increasing, then duties in their glory and acceptableness decay likewise.

10. This grace of fear is a grace that, if you abound therein, will give you great boldness both

with God and men. Job was a man, unique in his day in fearing God; and who was so bold with God and with men as he?

How bold was he with God, when he wished for nothing more than that he might come even to His seat, and concluded that if he could come to Him, he would approach even as a prince unto Him, and as such would present his cause before Him!

Also, before his friends, how bold was he! For even as they laid to his charge that he was a hypocrite, he repelled them with the testimony of a good conscience. This good conscience he got, kept, and maintained by increasing in the fear of God; yea, his conscience was kept so good by this grace of fear (for it was by that he fled evil) that it was common with him to appeal to God when accused, and also to put himself, to underscore his innocence, under the most bitter curses and imprecations.

This fear of God is what keeps the conscience clean and tender, and so free from much of that defilement that even a good man may be afflicted with for want of this growth in the fear of God.

Yea, let me add, if a man can, with a good conscience, say that he desires to fear the name of God, it will add boldness to his soul in his approaches into the presence of God. "O Lord," said Nehemiah, "I beseech Thee, let now Thine ear be attentive to the prayer of Thy servants who desire to fear Thy name" (Nehemiah 1:11). He pleaded his desire to fear the name of God as an argument with God to grant him his request; and the reason was that God had promised before to bless those who fear Him, both small and great.

11. By the fear of the Lord, and by growing in this fear, you may have your labors blessed to the saving of the souls of others. It is said that Levi (of whom mention was made before that he feared God, and was afraid before His name) saved others from their sins. "The law of truth was in his mouth, and iniquity was not found in his lips; and he walked with Me in peace and equity, and did turn many away from iniquity" (Malachi 2:6). The fear of God that dwelt in his heart showed its growth in the sanctifying of the Lord by his life and words; and the Lord also blessed his growth herein by blessing his labors to the saving of his neighbors.

Would you save your husband, your wife, your children? Then be greatly in the fear of God. This Peter teaches: "Wives, be in subjection to your own husbands, that if any obey not the word, they also may without the word be won by the conversation of the wives, while they behold your chaste conversation coupled with fear" (1 Peter 3:1–2).

So, then, if wives and children, yea, if husbands, wives, children, and servants did but better observe this general rule of Peter (namely of letting their whole conversation be coupled with fear) they might be made instruments in God's hand of much more good than they are. But the misery is that the fear of God is wanting in actions, and that is the cause why so little good is done by those who profess it. It is not a conversation that is coupled with a profession—for a great profession may be attended with a life that is not good, but scandalous—but it is a conversation coupled with fear of God, that is, with the impressions of the fear of God upon it, which is convincing, and which ministers the awakenings of God to the conscience in order to saving the unbeliever. Oh, they are a sweet couple, namely a Christian conversation coupled with fear!

The want of this fear of God is that which oftentimes has been a stumbling block to the blind. Alas, the world will not be convinced by your talk, by your ideas, and by the great profession that you make, if they see not therewith mixed the lively impressions of the fear of God! But they will, as I said, rather stumble and fall at your conversation, and at your profession itself. Wherefore, to prevent this mischief, that is, the stumbling of souls while you make your profession of God by a conversation not becoming your profession, God bids you fear Him—implying that a good conversation coupled with fear delivers the blind world from those falls from which otherwise they cannot be delivered. "Thou shalt not curse the deaf, nor put a stumbling block before the blind, but shalt fear thy God: I am the Lord" (Leviticus 19:14).

"But shalt fear thy God." That is the remedy that will prevent their stumbling at you, whatever else they stumble at. Wherefore Paul says to Timothy, "Take heed unto thyself, and unto the doctrine; continue in them, for in doing this thou shalt both save thyself, and them that hear thee" (1 Timothy 4:16).

12. The fear of God is the way to engage God to deliver you from many outward dangers into which you may fall.

This is proved from the history of the Hebrew midwives. "The midwives," says Moses, "feared God, and did not drown the male children, as the king had commanded, but saved them alive." And what follows? "Therefore God dealt well with the midwives, and the people multiplied, and waxed very mighty. And it came to pass, because the midwives feared God, that He made them houses" (Exodus 1:17, 20–21); that is, He sheltered them, and caused them to be hidden from the rage and fury of the king, and that perhaps in some of the houses of the Egyptians themselves; for why might not the midwives be hidden there as well as was Moses, even in the king's court?

And how many times are those who fear God said to be delivered, both by God and His holy angels, as I have already shown.

13. This is the way to be delivered from errors and damnable opinions. There are some who perish in their righteousness; that is an error. There are some who perish in their wickedness; and that is an error also. Some, again, prolong their lives by their wickedness, while others are overly self-righteous or overly wise; all these are snares, and pits, and holes. But then, you say, how shall I escape? Indeed, that is the question, and the Holy Ghost resolves it thus: "He that feareth God shall come forth of them all" (Ecclesiastes 7:18).

14. Another motive to fear, and to grow in this fear of God, is that those who fear God have leave, be they never so dark in their souls, to come boldly to Jesus Christ and to trust in Him for life. I told you before that those who fear God have, in general, a license to trust in Him. But now I tell you more specifically that they especially may do it, even

though in the dark. You who sit in darkness and have no light, if this grace of fear is alive in your hearts, you have this boldness. "Who is among you that feareth the Lord, that obeyeth the voice of His Servant, that walketh in darkness, and hath no light? Let him trust in the name of the Lord, and stay upon his God" (Isaiah 50:10).

It is no small advantage, you know, when men have to deal in difficult matters, to have a patent or license to deal. Now to trust in the Lord is a difficult thing, yet the best and most gainful of all. "But then," some will say, "since it is so difficult, how may we do it without danger?" The text gives a license, a patent, to those to trust in His name who have His fear in their hearts. "Let him trust in the name of the Lord, and stay upon his God."

15. God will own and acknowledge such to be His, whoever He rejects. Yea, He will distinguish and separate them from all others in the day of His terrible judgments.

He will do with them as He did with those who sighed for the abominations that were done in the land, commanding the man who had his inkhorn by his side to set a mark upon their foreheads that they might not fall in that judgment with others.

So God says plainly of those who feared the Lord, and who thought upon His name, that they should be written in His book: "A book of remembrance was written before Him for them that feared the Lord, and that thought upon His name. 'And they shall be Mine,' saith the Lord of hosts, 'in that day when I make up My jewels; and I will spare them, as a man spareth his own son that serveth him' "

(Malachi 3:16–17).

Mark, He both acknowledges them as His and also promises to spare them as a man would spare his own son. Yea, moreover, He will wrap them up as His chief jewels in the bundle of life.

How to Grow in the Fear of God

Having given you these motives to the duty of growing in this fear of God, before I leave this use I will, in a few words, show you how you may grow in this fear of God.

1. First, then, if you would grow in this fear of God, learn rightly to distinguish types of fear in general. I mean, learn to distinguish between fear that is godly and that which in itself is indeed ungodly fear of God; know them well one from the other lest the one, the fear that in itself is ungodly, gets the upper hand of that which truly is godly fear. And remember the ungodly fear of God is by God Himself counted an enemy to Him and hurtful to His people, and is therefore most plentifully forbidden in the Word.

2. If you would grow in this godly fear, learn rightly to distinguish it from that fear in particular that is godly but for a time, from that fear that is wrought by the Spirit as a Spirit of bondage. I say, learn to distinguish the two, and also perfectly to know the bounds that God has set to that fear that is wrought by the Spirit as a Spirit of bondage, lest, instead of growing in the fear that is to abide with your soul forever, you be overrun again with that

first fear which is to abide with you only till the Spirit of adoption comes. And that you may not only distinguish them one from the other, but also keep each in its due place and bounds, consider, in general, what has already been said on this topic, and, in particular, that the first fear is no more wrought by the Holy Spirit, but by the devil, to distress you, and make you to live not like a son, but a slave. And, for your better help in this matter, know that God Himself has set bounds to this fear, and has concluded that after the Spirit of adoption has come that other fear is wrought in your heart by Him no more.

Again, before I leave this, let me tell you that if you do not well settle yourself in this matter, this bondage-fear, namely that which is like godly fear, though not wrought in you by the Holy Ghost, will, by the management and subtlety of the devil, the author of it, haunt you, disturb you, and make you live uncomfortably, and that while you are an heir to God and His kingdom. This is that fear that the apostle speaks of that makes men subject to bondage all their lifetime (Hebrews 2:15).

For though Christ will deliver you indeed at last, you having embraced Him by faith, yet your life will be full of trouble; and death, though Jesus has abolished it, will be always a frightful object to you in all your ways and thoughts, breaking your peace and making you draw your loins heavily after Him.

3. Would you grow in this godly fear? Then as you should learn to distinguish between fears, so you should make conscience of which to entertain and cherish. If God would have His fear—and it is called

His fear by way of eminence: "That His fear may be
before you that you sin not" (Exodus 20:20)—I say, if
God would have His fear be with you, then you
should make conscience of this, and not so lightly
give way to slavish fear as is common for Christians
to do.

There is a fault among Christians about this
thing, that is, they make not that conscience of re-
sisting slavish fear as they should. They rather cherish and entertain it, and so weaken themselves and
that fear which they should strengthen. And this is
the reason why we so often lie struggling under the
black and amazing thoughts that are engendered in
our hearts by unbelief; for this fear nourishes unbelief, if we give way to it after the Spirit of adoption
has come, and readily close with all the fiery darts of
the wicked.

But Christians are ready to do with this fear as
the horse does when the spur is set against his side:
lean to it until it enters into his belly. We lean naturally on this fear, I mean, after God has done good
to our souls; it is hard striving against it because it
has our sense and feeling on its side.

But, I say, if you would be a growing Christian,
growing, I say, in the fear that is godly, in the fear
that is always so, then make conscience of striving
against the other, and against all these things that
would bring you back to it. "Wherefore should I
fear," said David, "in the days of evil, when the iniquity of my heels shall compass me about?" (Psalm
49:5).

What? Not fear in the day of evil? What? Not
when the iniquity of your heels surrounds you? "No,

not then," says he. That is, not with that fear that would bring him again into bondage to the law; for he had received the Spirit of adoption before. Indeed, if a Christian ever has ground to give way to slavish fear, it is at these two times: in the day of evil, and when the iniquity of his heels surrounds him. But you see David would not then give way thereto; nor did he see reason why he should. "Wherefore should I?" said he. Wherefore, indeed—since now you have become a son of God through Christ, and have received the Spirit of His Son into your heart, crying, "Father, Father."

4. Would you grow in this grace of godly fear? Then grow in the knowledge of the new covenant; for that is indeed the girdle of our reins and the strength of our souls. Hear what Zechariah says: "God hath raised up a horn of salvation for us in the house of His servant David, as He spake by the mouth of His holy prophets, which have been since the world began" (Luke 1:69–70). But what was it that He spoke? Why, "That He would grant unto us that we, being delivered out of the hand of our enemies, might serve Him without fear, in holiness and righteousness before Him, all the days of our life" (verses 74–75). But upon what is this princely, fearless service of God grounded? Why, upon the holy covenant of God, upon the oath that He swore to Abraham.

Now, in this covenant is wrapped up all your salvation; in it is contained all your desire. And I am sure, then, that it contains the complete salvation of your soul. And, I say, since this covenant is confirmed by promise, by oath, and by the blood of the

Son of God, and that on purpose so that you might serve your God without slavish fear, then the knowledge and faith of this covenant are of absolute necessity to bring us into this liberty and out of our slavish terrors, and so, consequently, to cause us to grow in that sonlike, godly fear which became even the Son of God Himself, and becomes all His disciples to live in the growth and exercise of it.

5. Would you grow in this godly fear? Then labor always to keep your evidences of heaven and your salvation alive upon your heart; for he who loses his evidences of heaven will hardly keep slavish fear out of his heart, but he who has the wisdom and grace to keep them alive, and apparent to himself, will grow in this godly fear. See how David words it: "From the end of the earth will I cry unto Thee when my heart is overwhelmed; lead me to the Rock that is higher than I. For Thou hast been a shelter for me, and a strong tower from the enemy. I will abide in Thy tabernacle forever; I will trust in the cover of Thy wings. For Thou, O God, hast heard my vows; Thou hast given me the heritage of those that fear Thy name" (Psalm 61:2–5).

By these words David suggests, first, that sometimes, to his thinking, he was as far off from his God as the ends of the earth are asunder, and that at such times he was subject to being overwhelmed, or afraid. Second, the way that he took at such times to help himself was to cry to God to lead him again to Jesus Christ: "Lead me to the Rock that is higher than I." For, indeed, without faith in Him, and the renewing of that faith, no evidence of heaven can be made to appear to the soul. This, therefore, he prays for first. Then he puts that faith into exercise, and that with respect to the time that was past, and also the time that was to come. For the time past, he says, "Thou hast been a shelter to me, and a strong tower from the enemy." And for the time to come he says, "I will abide in Thy tabernacle," that is, in Thy Christ by faith, and in the way of worship by love forever.

And observe, he makes the believing remembrance of his first evidences of heaven the ground of his cry and faith. "For Thou," he says, "O God, hast given me the heritage of those that fear Thy name." That is, "Thou hast made me meet to be partaker of the mercy of Thy chosen, and hast put me under the blessing of goodness wherewith Thou hast blessed those who fear Thee."

Thus you see how David, in his distresses, musters up his prayers, faith, and evidences of eternal life, that he might deliver himself from being overwhelmed with slavish fear, and that he might also abound in that sonlike fear of his fellow-brethren, which is not only comely with respect to our profession, but profitable to our souls.

6. Would you grow in this fear of God? Then set before your eyes the being and majesty of God; for that begets, maintains, and increases this fear. And hence it is called "the fear of God," that is, a holy and awful dread and reverence for His majesty; for the fear of God is to stand in awe of Him, but how can that be done if we do not set Him before us? Again, if we would fear Him more, we must abide more in the sense and faith of His glorious majesty. Hence this fear and God's name are so often put to-

gether: "Fear God," "Fear the Lord," "Fear your God," "Do this in the fear of the Lord," and "You shall fear your God, I am the Lord."

For these words, "I am the Lord thy God," and the like, are purposely put in not only to show us whom we should fear, but also to beget, maintain, and increase in us that fear that is due from us to that glorious and fearful name, the Lord our God.

7. Would you grow in this grace of fear? Then always keep close to your conscience the authority of the Word. Fear the commandment, as the commandment of a God both mighty and glorious, and as the commandment of a Father, both loving and full of pity. Let this commandment, I say, be always with your eye, with your ear, and with your heart; for then you will be taught not only to fear, but to *abound* in the fear of the Lord. Every grace is nourished by the Word, and without it there is no thrift in the soul.

8. Would you grow in this grace of fear? Then be much in the faith of the promise that makes over to your soul an interest in God by Christ, and in all good things. The promise naturally tends to increase in us the fear of the Lord, because this fear grows by goodness and mercy. "They shall fear the Lord and His goodness" (Hosea 3:5). Now, this goodness and mercy of God are wrapped up in and made over to us by promise; for God gave it to Abraham by promise. Therefore, the faith and hope of the promise cause this fear to grow in the soul. "Having therefore these promises, dearly beloved, let us cleanse ourselves from all filthiness of the flesh and spirit, perfecting holiness in the fear of God"

(2 Corinthians 7:1). To attain this "perfect holiness in the fear of God," that fear received by the promise must grow mighty, for by, with, and in it you see that holiness is perfected.

9. Would you grow in this grace of fear? Then remember the judgments of God that have overtaken or shall certainly overtake those professors who have either been downright hypocrites or else unwatchful Christians; for both these sorts partake of the judgments of God—the true Christian for his unwatchfulness, for his correction; the hypocrite for his hypocrisy, to his destruction. This is the way to make you stand in awe, and to make you tremble and grow in the grace of fear before your God.

QUESTION. "Judgments," you may say, "what judgments?"

ANSWER. Time would fail me here to tell you of the judgments that sometimes overtake God's people, and that always certainly overtake the hypocrite for his transgressions.

For those that attend God's people, I would have you look back to the place in this book where they are particularly touched upon.

And for those that attend the hypocrite, in general they are these: blindness of heart in this world, the death of their hope at the day of their death, and the damnation of their souls at the day of judgment.

The godly consideration of these things tends to make men grow in the fear of God.

10. Would you grow in this grace of fear? Then study the excellences of the grace of fear, and what profit it yields to those who have it. Labor to get your heart to love both the exercise of the grace itself and

the fruit it yields; for a man hardly grows in the increase of any grace until his heart is united to it, and until it is made lovely in his eyes.

Now, the excellences of this grace of fear have also been discussed in this book already, where, by reading, you shall find the fruit it bears and the promises that are annexed to it. Because they are many, I refer you there for your instruction.

11. Would you grow in this grace of fear? Then remember what a world of privileges belong to those who fear the Lord, namely that such shall not be hurt, shall want no good thing, shall be guarded by angels, and have a special license, though in ever so dreadful a plight, to trust in the name of the Lord and stay upon their God.

12. Would you grow in this grace of fear? Then be much in prayer to God for an abundance of the increase thereof. To fear God is that which is according to His will, and "if we ask anything according to His will, He heareth us" (1 John 5:14). Pray, therefore, that God would unite your heart to fear His name; this is the way to grow in the grace of fear.

13. Would you grow in this grace of fear? Then devote yourself to it. "Devote myself to it," you will say, "how do I do that?" I answer, give yourself to it; addict yourself to it; solace yourself in the contemplation of God, and in reverence for His name, Word, and worship. Then will you fear, and grow in this grace of fear.

Things That Hinder Growth in the Fear of God

And that I may yet be helpful to you, I shall now caution you regarding those things that will, if way is given to them, hinder your growth in this fear of God. Because they are very hurtful to the people of God, I would have you be warned of them:

1. If you would grow in this grace of fear, take heed of a hard heart; for that will hinder your growth in this grace. "Why hast Thou made us to err from Thy ways, and hardened our heart from Thy fear?" (Isaiah 63:17) was a bitter complaint of the Church heretofore; for it is not only the judgment that in itself is dreadful and sore to God's people, but that which greatly hinders the growth of this grace in the soul. A hard heart is but barren ground for any grace to grow in, especially for the grace of fear. There is little of this fear where the heart indeed is hard; nor will there ever be much therein.

Now, if you would be kept from a hard heart, take heed of the beginnings of sin. Take heed, I say, of that, though it should be ever so small. "A little leaven leavens the whole lump" (1 Corinthians 5:6). There is more in a little sin to harden than in a great deal of grace to soften. David's look upon Bathsheba was, one would think, but a small matter; yet that beginning of sin contracted such hardness of heart in him that it carried him almost beyond all fear of God. It carried him to commit lewdness with her, to murder Uriah, and to an abundance of wicked dissimulation. These things, I say, have a direct tendency to quench and destroy all fear of God in the soul.

If you have sinned, do not lie down without repentance; for the want of repentance after one has sinned makes the heart yet harder and harder.

Indeed, a hard heart is impenitent; and impenitence also makes the heart harder and harder. So that if impenitence is added to hardness of heart, or to the beginnings of sin which makes it so, it will quickly be with that soul as is said of the house of Israel: "Thou refusedst to be ashamed" (Jeremiah 3:3).

If you would be rid of a hard heart, that great enemy to the growth of the grace of fear, be much with Christ upon the cross in your meditations, for that is an excellent remedy against hardness of heart. A right sight of Him, as He hung there for your sins, will dissolve your heart into tears and make it soft and tender. "They shall look upon Me whom they have pierced, and they shall mourn" (Zechariah 12:10). Now, a soft, tender, and broken heart is a fit place for the grace of fear to thrive in.

2. If you would have the grace of fear grow in your soul, take heed also of a prayerless heart; for that is not a place for this grace of fear to grow in. Hence, he who refrains from prayer is said to cast off fear. "Thou castest off fear," said one of Job's friends to him. But how did he do that? Why, the next words show you: "Thou restrainest prayer before God" (Job 15:4). Do you see a professor who prays not? That man thrusts the fear of God away from him. Do you see a man who prays but little? That man fears God but little; for it is the praying soul, the man who is mighty in prayer, who has a heart for the fear of God to grow in. Take heed, therefore, of a prayerless

heart if you would grow in this grace of the fear of God.

Prayer is as the pitcher that fetches water from the brook, therewith to water the herbs: break the pitcher and it will fetch no water, and for want of water the garden withers.

3. Would you grow in this grace of fear? Then take heed of a light and wanton heart; for such a heart is not good ground for the fear of God to grow in. Wherefore it is said that Judah "feared not, but went and played the harlot also" (Jeremiah 3:8). She was given to wantonness, and to be light and vain, and so her fear of God decayed. Had Joseph been as wanton as his mistress, he would have been as devoid of the fear of God as she; but he was a sober, tender, godly, considerate spirit, and therefore he grew in the fear of God.

4. Would you grow in this grace of fear? Then take heed of a covetous heart; for that is not good ground for this grace of fear to grow in. Therefore, this covetousness and the fear of God are as enemies, set in opposition one against the other. "Such as fear God, men of truth, hating covetousness" (Exodus 18:21).

And the reason why covetousness is such an obstruction to the growth of this grace of fear is that covetousness casts those things out of the heart which alone can nourish this fear. It casts out the Word and love of God, without which no grace can grow in the soul. How, then, can the fear of God grow in a covetous heart?

5. Would you grow in this grace of fear? Then take heed of an unbelieving heart; for an unbeliev-

ing heart is not good ground for this grace of fear to grow in. An unbelieving heart is called "an evil heart" in Hebrews 3:12 because from it flows all the wickedness that is committed in the world. Now, it is faith, or a believing heart, that nourishes this fear of God, while an evil heart does not. The reason is that faith brings God, heaven, and hell to the soul, and makes it duly consider them all. This is, therefore, the means of fear, and that which will make it grow in the soul; but unbelief is a bane thereto.

6. Would you grow in this grace of fear? Then take heed of a forgetful heart. Such a heart is not a heart where the grace of fear will flourish. "When I remember I am afraid, and trembling taketh hold on my flesh" (Job 21:6). Therefore take heed of forgetfulness; do not forget, but remember God, and His kindness, patience, and mercy to those who yet neither have grace nor special favor from Him, and that will beget and nourish His fear in your heart. But forgetfulness of this, or of any other of His judgments, is a great wound and weakening this fear. When a man well remembers that God's judgments are so great and deep a mystery, as indeed they are, that remembrance puts a man upon such considerations of God and of His judgments as to make him fear. "Therefore," says Job, "am I troubled at His presence; when I consider, I am afraid of Him" (Job 23:15), that is, when he remembers and considers the wonderful depths of His judgments toward man.

7. Would you grow in this grace of fear? Then take heed of a murmuring and repining heart; for that is not a heart for this grace of fear to grow in.

For instance, when men murmur and repine at God's hand, at His dispensations, and at the judgments that overtake them in their persons, estates, families, or relations, their murmuring tends to destroy fear; for a murmuring spirit is such a one as seems to correct God, and to find fault with His dispensations. And where there is that, the heart is far from fear.

A murmuring spirit comes either from that wisdom that pretends to understand that there is a failure in the nature and execution of things, or from an envy and spite at the execution of them. Now, if murmurings arise from this pretended wisdom of the flesh, then, instead of fearing God, His actions are judged to be either rigid or ridiculous which are done in judgment, truth, and righteousness. Thus a murmuring heart cannot be a good one for the fear of God to grow in. Alas, the heart where that fear grows must be a soft one; as Job says, "God maketh my heart soft" (Job 23:16). It must be a heart that will stoop and be silent at the most abstruse of all His judgments: "I was dumb, I opened not my mouth, because Thou didst it" (Psalm 39:9).

The heart in which the fear of God flourishes is such that it bows and is mute if it can but see the hand, wisdom, justice, or holiness of God in this or the other of His dispensations, and so stirs up the soul to fear Him. But if this murmuring arises from envy and spite, that looks so like the spirit of the devil that nothing needs be said to give conviction of the horrible wickedness of it.

8. Would you grow in this grace of fear? Then take heed of a high and captious spirit; for that is

not good ground for the fear of God to grow in. A
meek and quiet spirit is the best, and there the fear
of God will flourish most. Therefore, Peter puts
meekness and fear together, as being most suited in
their nature and natural tendency one to another
(1 Peter 3:15).

Meekness of spirit is like that ground that has
depth of earth in it, in which things may take root
and grow; but a high and captious spirit is like the
stony ground, where there is not depth of earth, and
consequently where this grace of fear cannot grow.
Therefore, take heed of this kind of spirit if you
want the fear of God to grow in your soul.

9. Would you grow in the grace of fear? Then
take heed of an envious heart; for that is not a good
heart for the fear of God to grow in. "Let not thine
heart envy sinners, but be thou in the fear of the
Lord all the day long" (Proverbs 23:17). To envy any-
one is a sign of a bad spirit; and that man takes
upon him, as I have already hinted, to be a con-
troller and a judge, yea, and a malicious executioner
too, and that of the fury that arises from his own
lusts and revengeful spirit upon, perhaps, the man
who is more righteous than himself.

But suppose that he is a sinner who is the object
of your envy. Why, the text sets that envy in direct
opposition to the fear of God: "Envy not sinners, but
be thou in the fear of the Lord." These two, therefore, namely envy toward sinners and fearing of
God, are opposites. You cannot fear God and envy
sinners too. And the reason is that he who envies a
sinner has forgotten that he himself is as bad, and
how can he then fear God? He who envies sinners

rejects his duty of blessing of those who curse, and praying for those who despitefully use us. And how can he who has rejected this fear God? He who envies sinners, therefore, cannot be of a good spirit, nor can the fear of God grow in his heart.

10. Would you grow in this grace of fear? Then take heed of hardening your heart at any time against convictions to particular duties, such as to prayer, alms, self-denial, or the like. Take heed, also, of hardening your heart when you are under any judgments of God, such as sickness, losses, hardships, or the like.

I bade you before to beware of a hard heart, but now I bid you to beware of hardening your soft ones; for to harden the heart is to make it worse than it is, harder, more desperate, and bolder against God than at present it is. Now, I say, if you would grow in this grace of fear, take heed of hardening your heart, and especially of hardening it against convictions to good; for those convictions are sent of God like seasonable showers of rain to keep the tillage of your heart in good order, that the grace of fear may grow therein; but this stifling of convictions makes the heart as hard as a piece of millstone.

Therefore, happy is he who receives conviction, for so he stays in the fear of God, and that fear is thereby nourished in his soul. But cursed is he who does otherwise. "Happy is the man that feareth always; but he that hardeneth his heart shall fall into mischief" (Proverbs 28:14).

USE OF ENCOURAGEMENT. This use is for those who are blessed with this grace of fear. The last text that was mentioned says, "Happy is the man that feareth always," and so do many more. He is happy already because he is blessed with this grace; and he is happy for time to come because this grace shall abide and continue till the soul that has it is brought unto the mansion house of glory. "I will put My fear in their hearts, that they shall not depart from Me" (Jeremiah 32:40). Therefore, as here it says, "Happy is he," so it says also, "It shall be well with them," that is, in time to come. "It shall be well with them that fear God" (Ecclesiastes 8:12). Had God given you all the world, yet you would be cursed if He had not given you the fear of the Lord; for the fashion of this world is a fading thing, but he who fears the Lord shall abide forever and ever.

1. The first thing, therefore, that I would propound for your encouragement, O you who fear the Lord, is that this grace will dwell in your heart, for it is a new covenant grace, and will abide with you forever. It is sent to you from God not only to join your heart to Him, but to keep you from final apostasy. "I will put My fear in their hearts, that they shall not depart from Me" (Jeremiah 32:40). That you may never forsake God is His design; therefore, to keep you from that wicked thing, He has put His fear in your heart.

Many are the temptations, difficulties, snares, traps, trials, and troubles that the people of God pass through in the world; but how shall they be kept safe? How shall they be delivered and escape? Why, the fear of God will keep them. "He that feareth God shall come forth of them all" (Ecclesiastes 7:18).

Is it not, therefore, a wonderful mercy to be

blessed with this grace of fear, that by it you may be kept from final (which is damnable) apostasy? Bless God, therefore, you blessed man, who has this grace of fear in your soul.

There are five things in this grace of fear that have a direct tendency in them to keep you from final apostasy:

(1) It is seated in the heart; and the heart is, as I may call it, the main fort in the mystical world. It is not placed in the head, as knowledge is, nor in the mouth, as utterance is, but in the heart, the seat of all. "I will put My fear in their heart." If a king would keep a town secure for himself, let him be sure to sufficiently man the main fort thereof. If he has twenty thousand men well-armed, if they lie scattered here and there, the town may be taken despite all that; but if the main fort is well-manned, then the town is more secure. If a man had all the abilities, yea, all the arts of men and angels, they would not keep the heart for God. But when the heart, this principal fort, is possessed with the fear of God, then he is safe, but not otherwise.

(2) As with the heart in general, so the will in particular, that chief and great faculty of the soul, is the principal thing that is actuated by this fear.

Whichever way the will goes, all goes, whether it be to heaven or hell. Now, the will, I say, is that main faculty that is governed by this fear that possesses the soul. Therefore he says, "If ye will fear the Lord" (1 Samuel 12:14). Fearing God is a voluntary act of the will, and, that being so, the soul is kept from rebellion against the commandment because by the will—where this fear of God is placed and which it governs—all the other powers of the soul are led. In this will, then, is the fear of God placed so that this grace may the better be able to govern the soul, and so, by consequence, the whole man; for, as I said, look what way the will goes, look what the will does, and there goes and does the whole man.

When man's will is alienated from God, he is reckoned rebellious throughout, and that not without ground; for the will is the principal faculty of the soul as to obedience, and therefore things done without the will are as if they were not done at all. "The spirit is willing." "If ye be willing." "She hath done what she could." By these and such similar sayings, the goodness of the heart and action is judged as to the subjective part thereof.

Now, this fear that we have been speaking of is placed in the soul, and so, consequently, in the will, that the man may thereby the better be kept from final and damnable apostasy.

(3) This fear, as I may say, above every other grace, is God's well-wisher; and hence it is called, as I also have shown you, *His* fear. As He also says in the text mentioned before, "I will put My fear in their hearts." These words "His" and "My" are intimate and familiar expressions, speaking not only great favor to man, but delivering a very great trust to him. It is as if He should say, "This fear is My special friend; it will subject and bow the soul and the various faculties thereof to My pleasure; it is My great favorite, and subdues sinners to My pleasure." You shall rarely find faith, repentance, or abilities go under such familiar titles as this blessed fear of the Lord does. Of all the counselors and mighty men

that David had, Hushai alone was called the king's friend. So of all the graces of the Spirit, this fear of God goes mostly, if not always, by the title of "My fear," "God's fear," or "His fear."

As I said before, if the king will keep a town the main fort therein must be sufficiently manned. And now I will add that if he has no one to govern those men, some trusty and special friend such as Hushai was to David, he may find it lost when it should stand him in greatest stead. If a soul should possess all things that exist, yet, if this fear of God is wanting, all other things will give place in time of rebellion, and the soul shall be found in and under the conduct of hell when it should stand up for God and His truth in the world. This fear of God is God's special friend, and, therefore, it has given unto it the chief seat of the heart, the will, so that the whole man may now be, and also be kept hereafter, in the subjection and obedience of the gospel.

(4) This grace of fear is the softest and most tender for God's honor of any grace. It is that tender, sensible, and trembling grace that keeps the soul upon its continual watch. To keep a good watch is, you know, a wonderful safety to a place that is in continual danger because of the enemy. This is the grace that sets the watch, and that keeps the watchman awake.

A man cannot watch as he should if he is destitute of fear. Let him be confident and he sleeps; he unadvisedly lets into the garrison those who should not come there. Israel's fault, when they came to Canaan, was that they made a covenant with the inhabitants of the land, namely the Gibeonites, with-

out asking counsel of God. But would they have
done so, do you think, if at the same time the fear of
God had had its full play in the soul, in the army?
No, they at that time forgot to fear. The grace of fear
had not, at that time, its full stroke and sway among
them.

(5) This grace of fear is that which, as I may
say, first affects the hearts of saints with judgments
after we have sinned, and so is a beginning grace to
make right again that which by sin is put out of
frame. Oh, it is a precious grace of God! I know of
what I speak in this matter, and also where I would
have been long ago, through the power of my lusts
and the wiles of the devil, had it not been for the
fear of God.

2. Another encouragement for those who are
blessed with this blessed grace of fear is this: this
fear fails not to do this work for the soul if it is there
in truth, be it ever so small in measure. A little of
this leaven leavens the whole lump. True, a little will
not do, or help the soul to do, those worthy exploits
in the heart or life as well as a bigger measure
thereof. Nor indeed can a little of any grace do that
which a bigger measure will; but a little will preserve
the soul from final apostasy, and deliver it into the
arms of the Son of God at the final judgment.
Wherefore, when He says, "I will put My fear in their
heart," He does not say, "I will put so much of it
there, such a quantity, or such a degree," but, "I will
put My fear there."

I do not say this to in any way tempt the godly
man to be content with the least degree of the fear
of God in his heart. True, men should be glad that

God has put even the least degree of this grace into their souls; but they should not be content therewith. They should earnestly covet more, pray for more, and use all lawful means (that is, all the means appointed by God) that they may get more.

There are, as I have said, several degrees of this grace of fear; and our wisdom is to grow in it as in all other graces of the Spirit. The reasons why I have already shown you, and also the way to grow therein; but the least measure thereof will keep the soul from final apostasy. There are, as I have shown you, those who greatly fear the Lord, who fear exceedingly, and who fear Him above many of their brethren. But those who have little of this grace are saved as well as those who are great therein. "He will reward them that fear Him, small and great" (Revelation 11:18).

This fear of the Lord is the pulse of the soul, and as some pulses beat stronger and some weaker, so with this grace of fear in the soul. Those that beat best are a sign of life, but those that beat worst show that life is present. As long as the pulse beats we conclude that the man is not dead, though he is weak. And where this fear is, it preserves unto everlasting life.

There are pulses also that are intermittent, namely such as beat for a little, stop, and then beat again. These are dangerous pulses, but signs of life. This fear of God, also, is sometimes like this intermittent pulse: there are times when it forbears to work, and then it works again. David and Peter had an intermittent pulse, as did many other saints of God. I call that an intermittent pulse with reference to the fear we speak of, when there is some obstruction by the workings of corruptions in the soul, that is, some obstruction from and hindrance of the continual motion of this fear of God. Yet none of these, though they are various, and some of them may be signs of weakness, are signs of death, but life. "I will put My fear in their hearts, that they shall not depart from Me" (Jeremiah 32:40).

QUESTION. But you may ask, "How shall I know that I fear God?"

ANSWER. If I said that desires, true sincere desires to fear Him, are fear itself, I would not be speaking amiss. In natural things, a desire to be or do something does not make a man what he desires; for example, a sick, poor, or imprisoned man may desire to be well, to be rich, or to be at liberty, and yet be sick, poor, or in prison. Yet, in spiritual matters, a man's desire to be good, to believe, to love, to hope, and to fear God flows from the nature of grace itself.

I said before that in temporal things a man could not properly be said to be what he was not; yet, even in natural or temporal things, a man expresses his love for what he desires, whether it is health, riches, or liberty. In spiritual matters, sincere desires, such as love for a certain grace of God, flow from the root of the grace itself. "Thy servants, who desire to fear Thy name" (Nehemiah 1:11). Nehemiah rested himself before God upon this plea, that he desired to fear His name.

And hence, again, it is said concerning true desires, "The desire of a man is his kindness" (Proverbs 19:22); for a man shows his heart, his love, his affections, and his delights in his desires. And

since the grace of the fear of God is a grace so pleasant in the sight of God, and of so sanctifying a nature in the soul where it resides, a true, sincere desire to be blessed with that grace must flow from
some presence of this grace in the soul already.

True desires are lower than higher acts of grace,
but God will not overlook desires. "But now they desire a better country, that is, a heavenly one, wherefore God is not ashamed to be called their God; for
He hath prepared for them a city" (Hebrews 11:16).
Mark it! They desire a country, and they shall have a
city. At this low place, namely sincere desires, God
will meet the soul, and will tell him that He has accepted his desires, that his desires are His kindness
and flow from grace itself. "He will fulfill the desire
of them that fear Him" (Psalm 145:19). Therefore,
desires are not rejected by God; but they would be if
they did not flow from a principle of grace already
in the soul. Therefore, sincere desires to fear God
flow from grace which is already in the soul.

Therefore, since you fear God, and it is evident by
your desires that you do so, you are happy now in
this fear, and shall be happy forever hereafter in the
enjoyment of that which God, in another world, has
laid up for those who fear Him.

3. Another encouragement for those who have
this grace of fear is this: this grace can make that
man who in many other things is not capable of
serving God serve Him better than those who have
all else without it. Poor Christian man, you have
scarcely been able to do anything for God all your
days but to fear the Lord. You are no preacher, and
so you cannot serve Him that way; you are no rich

man, and so cannot serve Him with outward substance; you are no wise man, and so cannot do anything in that way. But here is your mercy: you fear
God. Though you cannot preach, you can fear God.
Though you have no bread to feed, nor fleece to
clothe the poor, you can fear God. Oh, how blessed
is the man who fears the Lord, because this duty of
fearing God is an act of the mind, and may be done
by the man who is destitute of all things except for
that holy and blessed mind!

Blessed, therefore, is that man, for God has not
laid the comfort of His people, nor the salvation of
their souls, in doing external duties, but in believing, loving, and fearing God. Neither has He made
these blessings depend on actions that require their
health, nor in the due management of their most
excellent abilities, but in receiving Christ and fearing God. Christian, you may do these things, and do
them acceptably, even though you should lie
bedridden all your days. You may also be sick and
believe, be sick and love, be sick and fear God, and
so be a blessed man.

And here the poor Christian has something to
answer those who reproach him for his ignoble
pedigree, or his limited attainment of the wisdom of
the world. "True," may that man say, "I was taken out
of the dunghill. I was born in a base and low estate,
but I fear God. I have no worldly greatness, nor excellence of natural parts, but I fear God."

When Obadiah met with Elijah, he gave him no
worldly and fantastic compliment, nor did he glory
in his promotion by Ahab, the king of Israel; but
gravely, and after a gracious manner, he said, "I thy

servant fear the Lord from my youth" (1 Kings 18:12). Also, when the mariners inquired of Jonah, saying, "What is thine occupation? and whence comest thou? what is thy country? and of what people art thou?" this was the answer he gave them: "I am a Hebrew, and I fear the Lord, the God of heaven, which hath made the sea and the dry land" (Jonah 1:8–9).

Indeed, this answer is the highest and most noble in the world, nor are there any, save a few, who in truth can thus express themselves, though of other answers they have enough. Most can say, "I have wisdom, or might, or riches, or friends, or health, or the like." These are common, and are greatly boasted in by most. But the man who fears God is he who can say, "I thy servant fear the Lord," when they say to him, "What are you?" He is the man among many; he is to be honored of men, though this, namely that he fears the Lord, is all that he has in this world. He has the thing, the honor, the life, and glory which are lasting. His blessedness will abide when other men's will be buried in the dust, in shame and contempt.

USE OF CAUTION. Hypocrites, my last word is to you! The hypocrite is one who would appear to be that in men's eyes that he is not in God's. You hypocrite! You would be esteemed as one who loves and fears God, but you do not. I have this to say to you: your condition is damnable, because you are a hypocrite and seek to deceive both God and man with guises, masks, shows, pretenses, and your formal, carnal, feigned subjection to the outside of statutes, laws, and commandments. But inside you are full of rottenness and all excess.

Hypocrite! You may, by cunning shifts, be veiled and hidden from men; but you are naked before the eyes of God. And He knows that His fear is not in your heart.

Hypocrite! Be admonished that no obedience is accepted by God where the heart is destitute of this grace of fear. Keeping the commandments is but one part of the duty of man, and Paul did that, even while he was a hypocrite. "Fear God, and keep His commandments; for this is the whole duty of man" (Ecclesiastes 12:13). But the hypocrite cannot "fear God," and therefore, as such, cannot escape the damnation of hell.

Hypocrite! You must fear God first, even before you offer to meddle with the commandments, that is, as to the keeping of them. Indeed, you should read therein that you may learn to fear the Lord; but to "fear God" goes before the command to keep His commandments. And if you do not fear God first, you transgress rather than keep the commandments.

Hypocrite! To "fear God" is that which the hypocrite quite forgets, although it is that which sanctifies the whole duty of man; for this is the one thing, and nothing else, that can make a man sincere in his obedience. The hypocrite looks for applause abroad, and forgets that he is condemned at home—and both of these he does because he lacks the fear of God.

Hypocrite! Be admonished that none of the privileges that are spoken of in the former part of this book belong to you, because you are a hypocrite. If you hope, your hope shall be cut off; if you lean upon your house, both you and it shall fall into hell-fire. Triumph? Your triumph is but for a while. Joy, then? "The joy of the hypocrite is but for a moment" (Job 20:5).

Perhaps you will not let go now of what, as a hypocrite, you have gotten. "What is the hope of the hypocrite, though he hath gained, when God taketh away his soul?" (Job 27:8).

Hypocrite! You should have chosen the fear of God, as you have chosen a profession of religion without it. But you have cast off fear because you are a hypocrite; and because you are such you shall have the same measure that you mete out. God will cast you off because you are a hypocrite. God has prepared a fear of God for you, because you did not choose the fear; and that fear shall come upon you like desolation, and like an armed man, and shall swallow you up, you and all that you are.

Hypocrite! Read this text and tremble: "The sinners in Zion are afraid; fearfulness hath surprised the hypocrites. Who among us shall dwell with the devouring fire? Who among us shall dwell with everlasting burnings?" (Isaiah 33:14).

Hypocrite! You are not under the fatherly protection of God because you are a hypocrite, and lack His fear in your heart. The eyes of the Lord are upon those who fear Him, to deliver them; but the fearless man is left to the snare and wiles of the devil, to be caught therein and overcome because he is destitute of the fear of God.

Hypocrite! You are likely to have no other reward

from God for your labor than that which the goats shall have. The hypocrite shall not stand in God's sight. The gain of your religion you spend as you get it; you will not have one farthing remaining at death and judgment.

Hypocrite! God has not entrusted you with the least drachma of His saving grace, nor will He, because you are a hypocrite. And as for what you have, you have stolen it, every man of you, from his neighbor, pilfering out of their profession, even as Judas did out of the bag. You came like a thief into your profession, and like a thief you shall go out of the same. Jesus Christ has not counted you faithful so as to commit to you any of His jewels to keep, because you fear Him not. He has given His banner to those who fear Him so that it may be displayed in truth.

Hypocrite! You are not true to God, nor man, nor your own soul, because you are a hypocrite. How should the Lord put any trust in you? Why should the saints look for any good from you? If God were to give you His word, you would sell it; if men were to commit their souls to you, you would destroy them by making merchandise of them for your own hypocritical designs. Yea, if the sun waxes hot, you will throw all away and not endure the heat, because you are a hypocrite.

Study Guide

Lesson 1: The Objects of and Reasons for Fear
(pp. 1–16)

"Blessed is every one that feareth the Lord, that walketh in His ways." Psalm 128:1 (KJV)
"The fear of the Lord is the beginning of wisdom." Proverbs 9:10 (KJV)

In this first lesson the objects of and reasons for the fear of God are examined. Though the Christian has the unbelievable privilege of being adopted into God's family, this filial relationship gives him no excuse for an unholy familiarity when addressing God. There exists such a reverential distance between the Creator and His creation that the angels in heaven recognize in their presence before Him (Isaiah 6:2). God is vastly superior to us in His omniscience, omnipresence, and omnipotence. He is the Creator; we are creatures. God is seated on His majestic throne in heaven, from which He sovereignly rules; and we dwell on His earthly estate. He is eternal and we are finite. He is perfect in holiness; we struggle with indwelling sin. And though God has made it possible for Christians to come before His infinite holy person, we must remember our approach is not based on our own merit, but we are accepted only by the righteousness of Christ imputed to us (2 Corinthians 5:21).

"Man crumbles to dust at the presence of God, though He shows Himself to us in His robes of salvation" (p. 4).

QUESTIONS:
1. Bunyan asserts that God is the Creator and Sustainer of all things. He then presents several reasons why it is our highest duty to fear God. What are some of these reasons?

The word "fear" is discussed in order to clarify its meaning as it is used in various passages of Scripture.

First we are to understand the word "fear" as a title for God Himself. Charles Spurgeon, in one of his sermons, refers to God as the "Dread Supreme." The people of God who have an informed view of God possess an adoration for His holy majesty, absolute power, and supreme otherness. Bunyan now presents three subjects which make God the fear of His people: God's presence, God's name, and God's worship.

2. God's presence is fearful. God's people have, as indicated by the use of the word fear in this context, an awe and reverence of His majesty not only in God's common presence but in His special presence. How did the men in the Scriptures cited react to an encounter with God?

3. There are three things that make His presence dreadful to us. They are:
        (1) To see God for who He is. How is He described?

(2) To see ourselves for what we are. How are we described?

(3) To see God's goodness. Why is the goodness of God a humbling and heartbreaking sight?

Bunyan describes "a company of poor, light, frothy professors in the world who carry on under the notion, which they call "the presence of God," but their behavior is more like antics than the behavior of sober, sensible Christians; yea, more like fools than those who feel the presence of God. How are we to express our solid and godly joy?

4. God's name is fearful. As a name distinguishes a person from another, so by God's name He is distinguished from His creation. In His name the nature of God is signified and His otherness expressed. What attributes of God are manifested by His name? Give verses.

5. As we see the attributes of God expressed in His name, why then is the name of God the object of a Christian's fear?

6. God has made it clear in Scripture that men are to show reverence and awe when they use His name. What demeanor should we expect when God's name is used in preaching, praying, and holy conversation?

7. God's worship is fearful. As the presence of God and the name of God are fearful, so is the worship of God. The worship of God occurs in the lives of Christians corporately on the Sabbath and from

there is expressed throughout the week.

Bunyan writes, "To praise God is a part of His worship." How this praise is expressed has often been debated. Regarding this issue, Jonathan Edwards, in his book *The Religious Affections* (Baker Book House, 1982, p. 281) states: "Hence gracious affections do not tend to make persons forward and noisy, but rather the contrary. Real Christians are disposed to clothe with a kind of holy fear all their behavior towards God and towards man. It becomes such sinful creatures as we are, to approach a holy God, although with faith and without terror, yet with contrition, penitence, and confusion of face."

In the contemporary vs. traditional worship debate, each side would proclaim their desire to reverence God in their worship. However, it would seem there is much equivocation regarding the word "reverence," especially when it is used with regards to worship style. Write a definition from the dictionary for the word "reverence."

8. Four things that make the worship of God a fearful thing are stated on pages 13–14. What are they, and what have you learned from each about how you should worship God?

9. It is stated that God's wrath and judgment are upon those who do not worship Him in fear. This rebukes three sorts of people.

(1) Name the first sort of people. Express why it is right that God's wrath is upon them.

(2) Name the second sort of people. List a few more wrong motives for worship, and then list some

legitimate ones.

(3) Name the third sort of people. The "Regulative Principle of Worship" states we only do in worship that which God expressly commands in Scripture. Do you think this would be helpful to correct the error of the third sort of people? How so?

The attitude that the third sort of people believe has led to cultural accommodation in worship. What are some possible dangers of this attitude?

Lesson 2: The Rule of Fear, and its Various Kinds
(pp. 17–40)

"...for Thou hast exalted above all things Thy name and Thy Word." Psalm 138:2b (KJV)

"...but to this man will I look, even to him that is poor and of a contrite spirit, and trembleth at My Word." Isaiah 66:2b (KJV)

In Lesson 1 we examined the word "fear" as it refers to God Himself, and specifically in His presence, His name, and His worship. We will now look at the word "fear" as it is taken for the Word of God. In Scripture, God has revealed to mankind His attributes, who we are and why we are here, His moral standard, and the plan of salvation for sinful mankind. This objective truth contained in God's Word should give us great cause to rejoice that God has initiated contact with rebels such as we, and tremble lest we slight or disregard His revealed will. Also in this lesson Bunyan will explain two sorts of fear that people naturally have at certain times, but they do not result in eternal life.

"All the beautiful objects in the world are not so lovely in the eye of God as a heart that trembles at the Word." (Jeremiah Burroughs, *Gospel Fear.* Soli Deo Gloria, 1991, p. 3)

QUESTIONS:
1. Bunyan states: "The written Word of God. . . ought to be the rule and directory of our fear" (p. 17). List some other standards that are used by Christians and non-Christians instead of God's Word.

2. According to Psalm 19:7-9, list some reasons given why the written Word of God is to be feared.

3. In a society that bases many of their opinions and actions on how they feel (subjectivism) about God and His Word, what does Bunyan say is the danger in this approach, and what alternative way is presented?

4. List some of the benefits given to a people who are described by God as "poor and of a contrite spirit, and trembleth at My Word."

5. The "dread and terror of the Word lieth in these things." Three things are discussed:
1) God as the Author of it. Why should there be dread and terror of the Word because God is the author?
2) The subject matter of it. The eternal matters that are dealt with in Scripture have been summarized as death, judgment, heaven, and hell. What

does scripture say about these topics that should cause sober reflection?

3) The truth and faithfulness of it. It is maintained that Scripture has truth that does not change from generation to generation or from culture to culture. What are the implications of this claim?

6. What are the consequences of lack of reverence for God's Word?

7. God's Word is the standard by which we may know the way of salvation or the way of condemnation. Some, however, reject this truth. "As for the Word of the Lord, it is nothing at all to them" (p. 23). To what other standard do they adhere instead?

8. Before Bunyan explains the type of fear of God "as it is a grace of the Spirit of God in the hearts of His people," he will address three sorts of fear of God that people at certain times naturally have. We will examine two of them in this lesson and the third one in lesson 3.

(1) A fear of God from the light of nature. How does he explain this?

(2) A fear of God from some of His dispensations to men yet it is neither universal, nor saving. This ungodly fear is described in several particulars. They are:

a. "The dread of God in His coming upon men to deal with them for their sins, is apprehended by them, and yet by this dispensation they have no change of heart to submit to Him thereunder" (pp. 26–27). What is the effect of this fear?

b. An ungodly fear "that drives a man away from God." From the examples given, why is this an ungodly fear? It is a fear forbidden because it causes what ill effects?

c. An ungodly fear that "even while they are in the outward way of God's ordinances, their hearts are by it quite discouraged from attempting to exercise themselves in the power of religion" (p. 32). Give an example and list the results of this fear.

d. An ungodly fear that "will not suffer the soul that is governed thereby to trust only to Christ for justification of life, but will bend the powers of the soul to trust partly to the works of the law" (p. 34). Man is prone to legalism and moralism because of his pride. "Pride is a big-bellied sin; most of the sins that are in the world are the offspring and issue of pride" (Richard Mayo, *Puritan Daily Devotional Chronicles*, Hearthstone Publishing Ltd., 1995, p. 227). How is pride expressed in this ungodly fear? What role does doubt have in this fear?

e. An ungodly fear which "will put men upon adding to the revealed will of God their own inventions, and their own performances of them, as a means to pacify the anger of God." What are some practices (give modern day examples if you can) that have been added to the revealed will of God? How could this fear be vanquished?

Lesson 3: A Third Sort of Fear Which Is Good and Godly, But Only for a Time
(pp. 40–66)

"For ye have not received a spirit of bondage again to fear; but ye have received the Spirit of adoption, whereby we cry, 'Abba! Father!' " Romans 8:15 (KJV)

In lesson 3 a third sort of fear is examined. It is a fear of God in some which is good and godly, but only for a time, until Christ, by the Spirit in the Word, is revealed to us, and we are made to accept Him by faith. Bunyan shows us what this fear is, by whom or what this fear is wrought in the heart, what this fear does in the heart, and when this fear is to have an end. Also examined are reasons why the Spirit of God cannot work this fear of damnation in the saved.

"Consider that He is good and has been good to you, good in that He has singled you out from others, and saved you from their death and hell, though you perhaps were worse in your life than those that He left when He laid hold on you. Oh how this should engage your heart to fear the Lord all the days of your life" (p. 66)!

QUESTIONS:
1. What does this fear cause a sinner to believe?

2. Bunyan states this fear is "wrought in the heart by the Spirit of God, working there at first as a Spirit

of bondage." What does this Spirit show us?

3. Bunyan lists six effects of this fear in the soul. What are they? In the majority of preaching today, which of these effects do you observe are stressed, and which ones do you think are not?

4. Give the three particulars which make this fear of damnation good. When does Bunyan say this fear becomes ungodly and should end?

5. What three reasons are given why the Spirit of God cannot work the fear of damnation in the saved.

6. Further reasons are requested to "convince me of the truth of what you say." They are:
    a. The work of the Spirit. Contrast the spirit of bondage with the Spirit of adoption.
    b. The covenant of grace. What assurances from the covenant of grace are mentioned to keep the child of God from the fear of damnation?
    c. Union with Christ. What are the benefits the believer has because of this union?

7. When the believer is brought into the fear of damnation, and into bondage by the spirit of the devil, the Christian may identify this by the groundlessness, unseasonableness, and effects of such fears. How do each of these hinder the Christian's faith?

8. The fear that the Spirit of God, as a spirit of

bondage, works in the soul of the Christian causes repentance. However, in this section, we will look at how this fear, when it comes to a person who has denied Christ, will cause him to run away from God.

a. To the ten questions asked, what is lacking in the answers?

b. Why are those in Christ not to receive the spirit of bondage again to fear when they sin? What distinctions are made between the sin of a child and that of a slave?

c. If a person uses the facts that the covenant cannot be broken nor the relation of Father and child dissolved to live as an antinomian, what would this reaction prove about this person?

9. Bunyan now gives thirteen considerations that God as a Father, by His rod and fatherly rebukes, can do to prevent antinomism in His children.

a. Which of the thirteen would you find to be most alarming and why?

b. What cautions are given if one has sinned and is under the high and mighty hand of God's chastisements?

10. What are some appropriate responses and attitudes to be learned from the four examples given (Job, David, Heman, the church in Lamentations) from the conduct of these saints under heavy afflictions for sin. (pp. 60-62)

11. List some of the ways the devil brings a child of God into the fears of damnation.

12. Indeed, the people of God should fear His rod, but not as a slave fears his master, but as a child fears his father. What will this type of fear cause in the heart of a child of God?

13. Five reasons are given to cause us to fear God with a child-like fear. Which of the five did you consider the best reason? Why?

Lesson 4: The True Character of the Fear of God
(pp. 67–82)

"Serve the Lord with fear, and rejoice with trembling." Psalm 2:11 (KJV)

In Lesson 2 we examined two fears that do not result in eternal life: a fear of God from the light of nature, and a fear of God from some of His dispensations to men; yet which is neither universal nor saving. In Lesson 3 it was a fear of God in some which is good and godly, but only for a time, until Christ, by the Spirit in the Word, is revealed to us, and we are made to accept Him by faith. In this lesson we will study the true character of the fear of God as it is described by the Scripture, and as it flows from God to His elect in various ways.

"By the fear of the Lord men depart from evil, that is, in their judgment, will, mind, and affections; not that by the fear of the Lord sin is annihilated, or has lost its being in the soul; there still will be those Cannaanites, but they are hated, loathed, abominated, fought against, prayed against, watched

against, strived against, and mortified in the soul"
(p. 72).

QUESTIONS:
1. This lasting godly fear is addressed by how the
Scripture describes it; first generally, and then more
particularly. Five general points are given:
Point 1. This Spirit of grace that is the author,
animator and maintainer of this fear enables us to
be subject to God's Word and ways. Describe in what
manner this subjection occurs.
Point 2. How does the second point say this fear
stands out?
Point 3. This godly fear is described as God's
treasure, His choice jewels. What do you think he is
referring to when he writes about "the scraps and
fragments that the poor vagrants obtain"?
Point 4. What does this grace of fear make men
do?
Point 5. What is the posture that results from this
fear? Explain the implications of this.

Then five particular points are given:
Point. 1. What does Bunyan say are the results of
a lack of this fear? How is this expressed in the way
we spend our time?
Point 2. Describe the wisdom that the fear of God
brings.
Point 3. How will men depart from evil because
of this fear of the Lord? What will still remain and
what is to be done? (see Romans 7)
Point 4. Why is this fear called a fountain of life?
Men in their pursuit of happiness often overlook

the source of "spiritual and eternal felicity." What is this source?

Point 5. The fear of the Lord is called "the instruction of wisdom." What is its tendency?

Next, Bunyan shows in eleven observations from where this fear of the Lord flows:

Observation 1. "This sonlike fear of God flows from the distinguishing love of God to His elect." It is wrapped up in a covenant. List some distinguishing features of His covenant.

Observation 2. Compare the actions and motivations that flow from a new heart with those that flow from a natural heart.

Observations 3 and 4 are linked together by the fact that "where the Word makes a sound impression on the soul, by that impression is faith begotten." What are the advantages to having the Word "engraven upon the face of our souls?"

Observation 5 and 6. What is the state and posture of one who has had a sound repentance worked in his soul?

Observation 7. What does God intend for the Christian to learn from the judgments He executes in the world?

Observation 8. Describe the scene at Horeb and how it should affect the soul.

Observations 9–11 are tied together by the fact that God is all-seeing. God sees our hearts and knows the turnings and returnings of them. What comfort should be drawn from this knowledge? What should be our response to the fact that God is an impartial judge?

Lesson 5: The Effects of Godly Fear
(pp. 83–102)

"The fear of the Lord is clean, enduring forever: the judgments of the Lord are true and righteous altogether." Psalm 19:9 (KJV)

In this section, Bunyan gives us the effects of godly fear. He does this by showing what flows from this godly fear of God when it is seated in the heart of man. Through the following fourteen points our vision will be enlarged to see God for who He is, decked in majesty and arrayed in splendor, and the practical implications thereof. May our reverence for His august being and our service to Him be enhanced through this lesson.

"For God expects that we serve Him with fear and trembling, and it is odious among men for a man, in the presence or about the service of his prince, to behave himself lightly and without due reverence of that majesty in whose presence and about whose business he is" (p. 88).

QUESTIONS:
1. The first effect is a devout reverence for God, and a concern for the glory due His name. List some of the examples given from Scripture. Can you think of some modern day counterparts to these examples?

2. This fear makes "them a watchful people." Of what are they watchful and why?

3. This fear causes reverential conversation "As evil communication corrupts good minds and manners, so good communication confirms them." (*Matthew Henry's Commentary on the Whole Bible*, Vol. 4, p. 1499) With this quote in mind, what was the topic of conversation the last time you were "with the saints in their religious and godly assemblies"? How did the conversation help your "further progress in the faith and way of holiness?"

4. It is claimed by some in our day that reverence is expressed in different ways in different cultures, therefore we are free to express ourselves before God in worship as our particular culture chooses to express reverence. What are the deficiencies in this argument? If in "the use and enjoyment of holy ordinances" we are walking in the "courts of heaven," where should we look instead for a definition of the way to express reverence?

5. This fear causes self-denial. What concerns did Nehemiah have for his brethren that caused his act of self-denial?

6. Perhaps no other standard is as easy to measure the grace of godly fear in our lives as that of singleness of heart. Often even our best deeds are a mixture of ulterior motives. "What's in it for me?" is the continual cry of our sinful nature. Scripture admonishes us to judge the motives of our hearts (Proverbs 4:23). What help did you receive from this section in your battle for singleness of heart?

7. Have you observed in today's church an example of compassion and caring for the saints in necessity and distress, even to the point of safety for life? Give an example.

8. What are the two fruits discussed in this section, and why are they inseparable?

9. It is stated: "Abraham had long before this [offering Isaac] done many a holy duty, and showed much willingness of heart to observe and do the will of God." How did this act of offering up Isaac differentiate from the other holy duties he had done?

10. The tenth effect of godly fear is humility of mind. Samuel Rutherford wrote to a friend, "Stoop, Stoop! It is a low entry to go in at heaven's gate." In order not to be high-minded, what are we to fear?

11. Hope in the mercy of God will cause a person to "a serious inquiry after that way of salvation which God Himself has prescribed." Where will he look, and what will be his reaction?

12. Bunyan makes the distinction that the use of means is not meritorious. Why, then, are we to engage in these means of grace?

13. Richard Sibbes has written that the motivation God desires in our obedience to His holy commands is that of "a free and a voluntary people, and not compelled unto Christ's service, otherwise than by the sweet constraint of love" (Richard Sibbes, *The*

Bruised Reed, Sovereign Grace Publishers, 1961, p. 55). What reasons does Bunyan give that there cannot be service to sin and the holy commands of God?

14. Where enlargement of heart is lacking, how does one serve God? Give an example of this.

Lesson 6 The Privileges of Those that Fear the Lord
(pp. 103–121)

"The fear of the Lord is the beginning of wisdom; a good understanding have all they that do His commandments. His praise endureth forever." Psalm 111:10 (KJV)

In the last lesson we examined the fourteen effects of fear. These effects of fear flow from the grace of fear rather than a promise to the person who has it, as will be the case in this lesson. We will now examine thirteen privileges of those who fear the Lord.

"Oh, how happy is the man who fears God! His good thoughts, his good attempts to serve Him, and his good life, please God because he fears Him. You know how pleasing the actions of our children are in our eyes when we know that they do what they do from a reverential fear and awe of us. Yea, though that which they do amounts but to little, we take it well at their hands and are pleased therewith" (p. 116).

QUESTIONS:

1. The first privilege is "that man who fears the Lord has a grant and a license to trust in the Lord, with an affirmation that the Lord is his help and his shield." What are the three enemies mentioned? Can you think of an example of how the Lord has been a help and a shield in combating these enemies in your own life?

2. "The devil leads men blindfolded to hell, but God enlightens men's eyes, sets things before them in a true light, and so leads them to heaven." (*Matthew Henry's Commentary on the Whole Bible,* Vol. 3, p.325) The devil misleads us, sinful man suppresses the truth in unrighteousness, and often we unwittingly lie to ourselves. What are some lies you have believed, and how has God been your blessed teacher and guide to enlighten your eyes?

3. A third privilege for those who fear the Lord is that God will open the secret of His covenant and of our concern in it. Thomas Shepard has described His covenant and our concern in it as follows: "The Father is glorious in His great work of election; the Son is glorious in His great work of redemption; the Holy Ghost is glorious in His work of application. The Father is glorious in choosing the house; the Son is glorious in buying the house; the Spirit is glorious in dwelling in the house" (*The Sincere Convert* and *The Sound Believer,* Soli Deo Gloria, 1991, p. 17). How does the thought of this cause "affecting ravishments" to your heart?

4. As a shepherd cares for his flock so "God's eye is always over you for good, to keep you from all evil." How is God like a good shepherd in caring for His sheep?

5. What are the advantages of those who fear God more and more, and how does this differ from the wicked people of the world?

6. In the sixth and seventh privileges Bunyan claims that "the angels, the heavenly creatures, have it in commission to take charge of them that fear the Lord." What proof does Bunyan give for this?

7. From the eighth privilege, list some of the distinctions made between mercy that is "nigh" them and mercy that is "upon" them.

8. Describe God's pity for those who fear Him, and the additional feature of it that is mentioned in the ninth privilege.

9. What is the desire of those who fear the Lord? List some of the characteristics of this desire.

10. The eleventh privilege is that God takes pleasure in those who fear Him. Since all that Christians do falls far short of God's perfect standard, and does not earn them merit for their salvation objectively, how does God take pleasure in the actions of His redeemed sinners?

11. Though fear may differ in degrees, it is the

same in nature. What are the three distinctions in definition that Bunyan gives for the word "small." Discuss some practical outworking of these thoughts.

12. List some comforts from the Psalm quoted in the text. List some comforts from some other portions of Scripture.

13. An objection is made that "perfect love casteth out fear" (1 John 4:18). Bunyan responds that fear "may be taken several ways." For the child of God, what types of fear should be cast out and what type of fear should remain?

Lesson 7: The Use of This Doctrine: An Examination of Ourselves Whether the Fear of God Is In Us Or Not.
(pp. 122–138)

"An oracle is within my heart concerning the sinfulness of the wicked: There is no fear of God before his eyes." Psalm 36:1 (NKJV)

In the last lesson, thirteen privileges of those who fear the Lord were examined. In this lesson, those who do not fear God will be considered in twelve propositions. This is done first by a self examination in general, then in particulars. The lesson will end with a consideration and two warnings to sinners to provoke the fear of the Lord. May the following thoughts be seriously considered by those who read them so they will not be found to be, as

Matthew Mead calls them, "almost Christians."

"They that fear God the least have the greatest reason to fear Him" (John Mason)

QUESTIONS:

Bunyan encourages us to examine ourselves to see if this grace (the fear of God) is in us. He does this by addressing the issue in general and in particular.

In general: "No man brings this grace into the world with him." Men may realize that God exists but do not show reverence for or worship of Him. Why do men remain strangers to this grace, the fear of God?

In particular. There are now given twelve propositions concerning those who fear not God.

1. "That man who is proud and of an high and lofty mind, fears not God." God has given various gifts to us that we may use them for His glory and for the good of others. However, as William Gurnall states: "Pride loves to climb up, not as Zaccheus to see Christ, but to be seen" (*A Puritan Golden Treasury,* Banner of Truth, 1989, p. 223). What will God do to the proud person? Have you seen an example of this?

2. "The covetous man fears not God." Spurgeon has written: "Pride meets covetousness, and compliments it as wise, thrifty, and prudent" (Charles Spurgeon. *The Treasury of David,* Thomas Nelson, 1985, Vol. 1, p. 111). So deceitful are our hearts that we are able to take the worst of sins and turn them into virtues. What warnings have you received from this section?

3. "The riotous eaters of flesh have not the fear of God." In modern day culture there is a great obsession to eat right. What are some wrong motives for this and what are some right motives?

4. "The liar is one who fears not God." Bunyan claims the sin of lying is a common sin and masquerades in several guises. What are some of them? Do you believe Rahab's lie (Joshua 2:4–6) is a guise for situational ethics?

Arthur Dent gives the questionable benefits of lying: "For by your willful and customary lying you gain inward grief, and lose true joy; you gain short pleasure, and lose perpetual glory; you gain hell, and lose heaven; you make the devil your friend, and God your enemy" (*The Plain Man's Pathway to Heaven*, Soli Deo Gloria, 1994, p. 130).

5. "Those fear not God who cry unto Him for help in the time of their calamity, and when they are delivered return to their former rebellion." Several abuses of God's mercies are given. How would any of them be true of you?

6. "Those fear not God who waylay His people, and seek to overthrow them, or to turn them besides the right path, as they are journeying from hence to their eternal rest." Their foolishness is shown by Thomas Manton: "A man's greatest care should be for that place where he lives longest; therefore eternity should be his scope" (*A Puritan Golden Treasury*, p. 92). What are some ways people seek to divert attention from eternal matters?

7. "Those fear not God who see His hand upon backsliders for their sins, and yet themselves will be backsliders also." What is the startling warning

given in this section?

"He falls deepest into hell who falls backward," said Thomas Manton.

8. "Those fear not God who can look upon a land wallowing in sin, and yet are not humbled at the sight thereof." Not only does the sin around them not bother them, what further sins do they commit?

9. "Those that take more heed to their own dreams than to the Word of God, fear not God." What tendency do thoughts from heaven have and what tendency do thoughts from Satan and the flesh have? Give examples.

10. "Those fear not God who are sorcerers, adulterers, false swearers, and who defraud the hireling of his wages." If their conscience does not judge them now, who will judge "in their day of account?" Can you imagine the excuses that they use? List some.

11. "Those fear not God who, instead of pitying, rail at God's people in their afflictions, temptations, and persecutions, and rather rejoice and skip for joy, than sympathize with them in their sorrow." What reasons are given for this rejoicing at God's people in their afflictions?

12. "Those that fear not God who are strangers to the effects of fear." Can you remember some of the effects of godly fear (from lesson 5) that are lacking in those who fear not God? List some.

List and describe some of the false fears that are now given.

This section ends with a consideration and two

warnings to provoke the fear of the Lord. What are they? Explain how you might use these in talking to a sinner who has cast off fear.

"The reason why so many fall into hell is because so few think of it" (John Mason).

Lesson 8: The Use of This Doctrine: An Exhortation to the Saints to Fear God, Part I
(pp. 138–152)

"The fear of the Lord tendeth to life, and he that hath it shall abide satisfied; he shall not be visited with evil." Proverbs 19:23 (KJV)

This section of the book ("The Use of This Doctrine: An Exhortation to the Saints to Fear God") will be examined in the next three lessons: Lesson 8 will show that the fear of God is a saving grace which is capable of being stronger or weaker. Thus fifteen motives are given to strengthen our fear of God. Lesson 9 gives us thirteen ways to grow in this fear of God. Lesson 10 lists ten hindrances to the growth of this grace.

In the following section, Bunyan points out that the fear of God is a grace of the new covenant which all Christians have. The following motives are given to cause believers to fear God more and more.

"Most people think that those are happy who never fear; but there is a fear which is so far from having torment in it that it has in it the greatest satisfaction. Happy is the man who always keeps up in his mind a holy awe and reverence of God, His glory, goodness, and government, who is always afraid of offending God and incurring His displeasure, who keeps conscience tender and has a dread of the appearance of evil, who is always jealous of himself, distrustful of his own sufficiency, and lives in expectation of troubles and changes, so that, whenever they come, they are no surprise to him. He who keeps up such a fear as this will live a life of faith and watchfulness, and therefore happy is he, blessed and holy" (*Matthew Henry's Commentary on the Whole Bible,* Vol. 3, p. 954).

QUESTIONS:

The examples of Obadiah, Job, and Hananiah show that they were men who feared the Lord greatly. Thus fifteen motives are given to encourage and strengthen the fear of God in the saints.

1. The first motive is God's distinguishing love to you. "Great gifts naturally tend to oblige, and will do so, I trust, with you when you shall ingenuously consider it." (p. 140) How should this obligation to thankfulness and gratitude be expressed?

2. The second motive is the privileges that this grace, the fear of God, lays you under. "It seems to me as if this grace of fear is the darling grace, the grace that God sets His heart upon at the highest rate" (p. 140). Why do you think God values this "darling grace" so highly?

3. The third motive is "the man who grows in this grace of the fear of the Lord will escape those evils into which others will fall." From the example of the healthy child who is careless, think of some stumblings, burns, and nearly drownings that the fear of God will keep you from.

4. The fourth motive to grow in this grace is that it will keep you in a conscientious performance of Christian duties. In the example of the watch, what remedy is given, and what is the practical out working of this regarding our Christian example?

5. The fifth motive is that it is a way to be wise. While head knowledge is greatly to be desired, if it only remains there and does not affect our life there is a problem. As Matthew Henry states: "A great understanding those have that know God's commandments and can discourse learnedly of them, but a good understanding have those that do them and walk according to them" (*Matthew Henry's Commentary on the Whole Bible,* Vol. 3, p. 664). How does Bunyan say wisdom is to be expressed?

6. The sixth motive to grow in the fear of God is "it is seemly for saints." Give some reasons why it is legitimate and fitting that Christians should reverence God because He is their Creator, King, and Father.

7. The seventh motive is "it is honorable to grow in this grace of fear." Bunyan claims the fear of the Lord is a sign of a princely spirit. Describe the way this "princely spirit" thinks and then acts.

"By the fear of the Lord men depart from evil; by the fear of man they run themselves into evil," said John Flavel.

8. The eighth motive is "This fear, and the increase of it, qualifies a man to be put in trust with heavenly and spiritual things, yea, with earthly things too." What are the reasons given that God will entrust a person that fears Him with spiritual matters? with earthly matters?

9. The ninth motive is "Where the fear of God in the heart of any is not growing no grace thrives, nor duty done as it should be." How does this lack of godly fear make faith, hope and love weak and the works that flow from them to be done poorly?

10. The tenth motive is "This grace of fear is a grace that, if you abound therein, will give you great boldness both with God and men." What argument and reasons does Nehemiah present before God? Take this example to present a current prayer request to God.

11. The eleventh motive is "By the fear of the Lord, and by growing in this fear, you may have your labors blessed to the saving of the souls of others." Have you ever read a book or attended a class on witnessing that stressed this truth? What are some of the implications of this concept to our witnessing?

12. The twelfth is "The fear of God is the way to engage God to deliver you from many outward dangers, whoever falls therein." How was this true in the midwives' actions?

"Where the fear of God rules in the heart, it will preserve it from the snare which the inordinate fear of man brings" (*Matthew Henry's Commentary on the Whole Bible,* Vol. 1, p. 273). Is there a situation in your life to which you should apply this principle?

13. The thirteenth is "This is the way to be delivered from errors and damnable opinions." Think of some "errors and damnable opinions" which are taught in present times. How would the fear of God enable one to discern these falsehoods?

14. The fourteenth is that "those who fear God have leave, be they never so dark in their souls, to

come boldly to Jesus Christ to trust in Him for life."
Do you think where this reverence and awe for God
is lacking that perhaps they have created a god of
their own imagination? What would be a remedy to
this problem?

15. The fifteenth motive is "God will own and acknowledge such to be His, whoever He rejects." If
your actions and words of this past week were written in this "book of remembrance," would God regard them as something to be remembered and
treasured?

**Lesson 9: The Use of This Doctrine: An Exhortation
to the Saints to Fear God, Part II**
(pp. 152–160)

"And now, Israel, what doth the Lord thy God require of thee, but to fear the Lord thy God, to walk
in all His ways, and to love Him, and to serve the
Lord thy God with all thy heart and with all thy
soul." Deuteronomy 10:12 (KJV)

In the last lesson, fifteen motives were given to
strengthen our fear of God. In this lesson, thirteen
ways will be examined in order to show how we may
grow in the fear of God. While God has provided
ways we may use to grow in this grace, we recognize
that it is only by the Holy Spirit's encouraging, en-
abling, and enlightening that we are able to grow in
spiritual matters. As Jonathan Edwards has directed:
"The more you have of a rational knowledge of divine things, the more opportunity will there be,
when the Spirit shall be breathed into your heart, to

see the excellency of these things, and to taste the sweetness of them" (*The Works of Jonathan Edwards*, Banner of Truth, 1990, Vol. 2, p. 162).

"Every grace is nourished by the Word, and without it there is no thrift in the soul" (p. 158).

QUESTIONS:

1. From the section of this book on ungodly fear, make the distinction in general between "fear that is godly, and that which in itself is indeed ungodly fear of God."

2. If we are to grow in the correct fear of God, we must be able to recognize fear that comes from the Spirit as a spirit of bondage which is used of God until the Spirit of adoption comes. How will confusion in this area "haunt, disturb, and make you live uncomfortably"?

3. How does cherishing and entertaining slavish fear weaken a Christian? When are we especially vunerable to it?

4. We are exhorted to grow in the knowledge of the new covenant. From this holy covenant, list what is contained in it for the complete salvation of the soul.

5. When David was overwhelmed, how did he keep his evidences for heaven and salvation alive in his soul?

6. God is an infinitely perfect Being who sits

upon His throne in heaven, garbed in grandeur and worshipped by the heavenly hosts. Name some attributes of God that should maintain and increase our fear of God.

7. God, as Creator and Owner of all, has the authority to rule and command His creation. As a Father He desires what is best for His children, and gives us rules to live by for our benefit, which are found in Scripture. What actions are therefore reasonable for one to take in view of these thoughts?

8. Explain the statement, "The promise naturally tends to increase in us the fear of the Lord, because this fear grows by goodness and mercy."

9. For what purpose do God's judgments come to the Christian? What are the judgments of God upon the hypocrite?

10. In points 10 and 11 Bunyan writes that, in order to grow in the fear of God, we should study the excellencies of this grace and remember the privileges of it. Thomas Chalmers has said, "There are two ways to displace from the human heart its love of the world—either by a demonstration of the world's vanity, so as that the heart shall be prevailed upon simply to withdraw its regards from an object that is not worthy of it, or by setting forth another object, even God, as more worthy of its attachment, so as that the heart shall be prevailed upon not to resign an old affection which shall have nothing to succeed it, but to exchange an old affection for a

new one" (Thomas Chalmers. *Twenty Centuries of Great Preaching: An Encyclopedia of Preaching* (Waco: Word Books, 1971), Vol. 3, p. 300). What are some excellencies of this grace that will attach your heart to it?

11. In points 12 and 13, Bunyan encourages the use of prayer, study of Scripture, and worship as a way of growing in the fear of God. How much time have you used this week to do these? From the time spent, do you expect to be increasing in this grace?

Lesson 10: The Use of This Doctrine: An Exhortation to the Saints to Fear God, Part III
(pp. 160–167)

"Happy is the man that feareth alway; but he that hardeneth his heart shall fall into mischief." Proverbs 28:14 (KJV)

Bunyan now gives ten things that have a tendency in them to hinder the growth of the fear of God in our hearts. As we would warn our own family or friends of the danger of an oncoming tornado, so Bunyan warns believers of the danger of the following sinful attitudes and actions that will limit the fear of God in saints.

"Prayer is as the pitcher that fetches water from the brook, therewith to water the herbs: break the pitcher and it will fetch no water, and for want of water the garden withers" (p. 163).

QUESTIONS:
1. A hard heart is the first hindrance. Bunyan gives three suggestions to keep our hearts from be-

ing hardened.

    a. His first suggestion involves David and Bathsheba. How would the following warning given by Spurgeon have helped David (and ourselves)? "We all see in nature how easily we may prove this, that little things lead to greater things. If it be desired to bridge a gulf, it is often the custom to shoot an arrow, and cross it with a line almost as thin as film. That line passes over and a string is drawn after it, and after that some small rope, and after that a cable, and after that the swinging suspension bridge, that makes a way for thousands. So it is oftentimes with Satan. It is but a thought that he would shoot across the mind. That thought shall carry a desire; that desire a look; that look a touch; that touch a deed; that deed a habit; and that habit something worse, until the man, from little beginnings, shall be swamped and drowned in iniquity. Little things, we say, lead on to something worse" (*Park Street Pulpit*, Vol. 5, p. 186).

    b. How would the last two suggestions keep a heart from hardness?

    2. A prayerless heart is the second hindrance. The lack of time spent in prayer is a struggle that even the most mature of Christians face. John Newton has confessed: "I find in my own case an unaccountable backwardness to pray. I can read, I can write, I can converse with a ready will, but secret prayer is far more spiritual than any of these. And the more spiritual any duty is the more my carnal heart is apt to start away from it" (John Newton, quoted in Alexander Whyte's *Thomas Shepard, Pilgrim Father and Founder of Harvard*, Oliphant, Anderson,

and Ferrier, 1894, p. 56). Why is prayer absolutely indispensable to the Christian?

3. A third hindrance is a light and wanton heart as exemplified in Israel and Potiphar's wife. "Let not that man think he makes any progress in holiness who walks not over the bellies of his lusts. He who doth not kill sin in his way takes no steps towards his journey's end" (John Owen, *Temptation and Sin,* Sovereign Grace Publishers, 1971, p. 14). How did Joseph kill sin and combat a wanton and light heart?

4. A fourth hindrance is a covetous heart. Why is covetousness such an obstruction to the growth of this grace of fear? What are the implications of this vacuum which is created?

5. A fifth hindrance is an unbelieving heart. Bunyan advocates faith as a means of nourishing the fear of God because it causes a consideration of eternal matters. How do people avoid the consideration of the four last things: death, judgment, heaven, hell, and therefore encourage an unbelieving heart?

6. A sixth hindrance is a forgetful heart. The Puritan Thomas Shepard confessed that his mind was a "bottomless bucket," so disposed was he to forgetfulness. What should be remembered about God in order to advance this grace of fear?

7. A seventh hindrance is a murmuring and repining heart. What pretentious thoughts flow from a murmuring and repining heart? How does a heart that fears God respond to all God's dispensations?

8. An eighth hindrance is a high and captious spirit. In considering a meek spirit as compared to a

high and captious spirit, an illustration of two types of soil is given. Describe the "things" (dispositions, traits, characteristics) that will grow out of each.

9. A ninth hindrance is an envious heart. Why are the "envy to sinners and fearing of God" opposites?

10. A tenth hindrance is hardening your heart at any time against convictions to particular duties, as to prayer, alms, self-denial, and the like. How are the "convictions of God to good" like "seasonable showers of rain?"

Lesson 11: The Use of This Doctrine: An Encouragement to Those who Fear God
(pp. 167–180)

"Though a sinner do evil an hundred times, and his days be prolonged, yet surely I know that it shall be well with them that fear God, which fear before Him." Ecclesiastes 8:12 (KJV)

In this final lesson, Bunyan gives several reasons why a person will be blessed in this life, as well as for eternity, if he has this grace of the fear of God. He gives five things which have a tendency in them to keep men from final apostasy, and gives encouragement even though this fear may be small. The book ends with dire warnings to the hypocrite.

"If a soul should be possessed with all things possible, yet if this fear of God is wanting, all other things will give place in time of rebellion, and the soul shall be found in, and under the conduct of hell when it should stand up for God and His truth in the world" (p. 171).

QUESTIONS:
A person is blessed if he has this grace of the fear of God because:

REASON 1. This fear of God is of eternal benefit as compared to the fashion of the world which is temporal. God's purpose is that Christians may never forsake Him, though many are the temptations, difficulties, snares, traps, trials, and troubles that Christians will have in this world.

There are five things in this grace of fear that have a direct tendency in them which will keep you from final apostasy. They are:

(1) The fear of God has been placed in the heart to protect it. "Heart," as it is used here, should be defined as including our mind, affections, and will, the inner person or soul. What will be our reaction to all sorts of providences when God has placed this fear in our hearts?

(2) The fear of God has been placed in the heart in general, and the will in particular. How does this fear of God in the will lead the rest of the powers of the soul?

(3) The fear of God, even above every other grace, is God's well-wisher. Why is this grace called God's well-wisher and God's special friend?

(4) The fear of God is the softest and most tender of God's honor of any grace. What are the advantages to this grace?

(5) The fear of God is that which first affects the hearts of saints with judgments, after we have sinned, and so is a beginning grace to bring again

to rights that which sin has put out of frame. What do you think are some of the "judgments" which affect the hearts of saints thus bringing them back to a correct frame?

REASON 2. This fear fails not to do this work of encouragement for the soul even if it is small in measure. What proofs does Bunyan give for this assertion in the example of the pulse? in the example of desires?

REASON 3. This fear can make that man, who in many other things is not capable of serving God, serve Him better than those who have all without it. Why is this true especially in regard to our sanctification?

Bunyan ends this book with a warning to hypocrites. Summarize the admonitions that are given to the hypocrite.